STREET SMARTS

Alonzo Weston

A Collection of Columns
Published in the St. Joseph News-Press

Amazing Things Press

Book design by Julie L. Casey

ISBN 978-0692598665
Printed in the United States of America.

For more information, visit
www.amazingthingspress.com

Dedicated to my mom,
Florestine Turner

Introduction

I wanted to be an artist first. I wouldn't say that I was afraid of words, but I stuttered terribly as a youth so I never really trusted them.

Where words failed me, art became my savior. I could communicate better through drawing and pictures. Besides, pictures spoke louder than words anyway and I wanted to be heard.

I'd watch family and friends grimace whenever I struggled with words in speech. I saw how it tested their patience in waiting for me to utter a simple sentence. Others however were not as kind or as patient and would ridicule me, not caring what I had to say. To them I was dumb.

With drawing and painting, I found I could communicate in pretty pictures. Those who ridiculed me began to give me some respect.

I can't remember when the desire to speak with pictures changed to wanting to communicate with the written word. I suspect maybe I remembered how I came from family of storytellers. I listened to my great-grandmother, grandmother, mother, aunts and uncles tell stories in colorful, descriptive language from our front porch on hot summer nights. I remember how my great-grandmother would make up bedtimes stories to put me to sleep at night.

For years I never pursued my passion for writing. I worked several laborer jobs before the St. Joseph News-Press gave me an internship in 1989. For that I'm forever grateful to the News-Press for allowing me to realize my dream of becoming a writer.

This collection of columns that I've written for the St. Joseph News-Press reflects my experiences growing up and living in St. Joseph and my observations and experiences as a reporter as well as just from being a contemplative member of society.

Former editor Bill Scott told me to "write for the guy in the pickup truck." I took that advice to heart. And in my heart lives the storytelling spirit of my family sitting on my Grandma Lena's porch on those hot sultry nights long ago.

God bless my folks for giving me a story telling gift. God bless the readers who thought my columns were special enough to vote me the city's favorite columnist for the past several years.

Bless the ones who didn't too.

Black Archives Museum

The African American story in Buchanan County is that of a deeply-rooted community with a largely forgotten history, that subtly negotiated its place in St. Joseph society. The Black Archives Museum showcases and serves as a repository for African American history for St. Joseph and the surrounding area. Originally known as the Knea-Von Black Archives, it was founded in 1991 by Jewell Robinson at 1901 Messanie. The Black Archives Museum became a member museum of the St. Joseph Museums, Inc. in 2001. Today its exhibits and public programs are located at the St. Joseph Museum's complex at 3406 Frederick Avenue in St. Joseph, Missouri. Proceeds from the sale of this book help support the mission of the Black Archives Museum.

FRIENDS & FAMILY

Plastic-covered 'living room' was hallowed ground in home

My parents have this space in their home called the Living Room, but no one ever lives in there. Everything's unused and covered in plastic, only to be used for special occasions like Christmas and family meetings. Only the best stuff in the house goes in the Living Room.

I know it's something serious when I go to my folk's house and see them sitting in this room, and it ain't Christmas. Either I have done something or my brother has. The Living Room is hallowed ground. You have to bow, curtsy, and take off your shoes before you enter. Plastic runners lead from the doorway to the couch and chairs. It's a family felony if you veer off course. Even the flowers are plastic, and all the furniture remains untouched by human hands, except those of the delivery man, and at times, my brother, Henry.

As a kid, I never dishonored the Living Room. I would walk around it in fear and reverence for all the sacred and fancy stuff that spent years on layaway.

A delivery man once told me that the furniture in his store would actually talk and dream of going to the Weston house to stay.

They would actually brag, if my mom put them on layaway.

"Nyah, nyah, nyah, after a couple of years on layaway, I'm going to the Westons' and have a place of honor in their Living Room," said one recliner to another.

"You my friend, will probably wind up as a beast of burden for some 400-lb. beer-swilling, food-dropping slob and end up at the city dump in six months."

But nothing in the Living Room was sacred to Henry.

As a kid, I remember the plastic would actually wilt when he walked by. No furniture was immortal in his eyes.

He once committed the sacrilege of all sacrileges by toting a BB gun into the Living Room, which to mom was on a level with cursing in church. As luck, or my brother's irreverence, would have it, the gun accidentally discharged. With all that plastic on everything, the BB didn't stop ricocheting for hours. When the BB finally did stop, the Living Room looked like a huge version of one of those plastic, grocery store bags with holes in it that grapes come in.

Needless to say, my brother was banned from the Living Room. All the conversations from Christmas activities and family meetings were piped to him in the basement. He could always be reached by walkie-talkie, until he was 30.

I swore I'd never have a Living Room when I got a home of my own, and now that I do, I have kept my word. We actually live in every room of our house. We don't use plastic anywhere, not even plastic cups.

And, furniture hates to come to my house.

At age 12, contentment was cheap and fit inside a grocery bag

Contentment costs too much nowadays. I'm not talking about the contentment you get from God, your marriage, from working in your garden or from sitting on your front porch. That's all still free—or it's supposed to be anyway.

And I'm not talking about our national contentment either. We all know that we lost that particular comfort for a while because of the September 11 terrorist attack.

No, the type of contentment that I'm talking about is the kind that comes from needs and wants and usually costs money. It's mostly about the cash you have to put out in order to get that neat sense of fulfillment and comfort.

For example, this type of contentment, at its basic level, consists of things like having your bills all caught up, a car that runs and the ability to pay for a weekend dinner and a movie.

Sure, there are folks who want nothing less than a new SUV or an in-ground swimming pool. I don't fault them for their materialism. If I could afford those things, I'm sure I'd probably feel that much more content and secure, too.

I just know that my contentment cost a whole lot less when I was 12 years old. Back then it only took a Spider-Man comic book, a Hostess Cupcake and a 3 V Cola to keep my world spinning.

There was never a shortage of work. I could always find enough grass to cut and enough errands to run so I could earn enough money to afford these things. And for me these three things were always good enough.

When I was 12, I was old enough to drink a big, 16-ounce 3 V Cola all by myself but I wasn't old enough to start feeling guilty about reading comic books yet. At 12 years old, I wasn't old enough for cupcakes and other sweets to be bad for me.

I was also lucky to have Uncle PeeWee who never outgrew comic books.

You could buy eight comic books and pay tax with a dollar then. I would get Uncle PeeWee four of the western type comics he liked, such as Kid Colt and the Two-Gun Kid, and I would get four super-hero comics. I was into Spider-Man pretty heavy but I liked the Incredible Hulk and the Fantasy Four, too.

Sometimes I had enough money in my pocket to buy a 3 V Cola and a Hostess Cupcake to go with the comic books. And if I did, my day would be complete. All that I lived for and all that I ever wanted fit in that brown paper sack from Jake's Drug Store. I would come home and spill it all on the dining room table. And that's where we would sit, my Uncle PeeWee and me, all afternoon listening to the rain on the roof and reading comic books. He would have his coffee and cigarettes. I would have my cupcakes and soda pop.

I knew only of a few things in this world that taste as good as a Hostess Cupcake washed down with a big 16-ounce 3 V Cola. I couldn't find much to compare with that feeling I got from drinking the soda pop so fast that it made my eyes water either.

Every so often I think it would be nice if I could regain those three simple things again. And all it usually takes to jolt me back to reality is a trip to any convenience store. They don't make 3 V Cola anymore. Most soda comes in 16-ounce bottles now. The sugar in cupcakes can kill me now because I'm a diabetic and the price of one comic book could kill my wallet.

Contentment may never be as cheap for me again as it was when I was 12 years old but I'm happy if I can still find it.

An uncle's job as role model isn't a thing that can be forced

I usually watch nothing on TV because at least I can understand the rules. I have trouble understanding how the folks on Jerry Springer, the TV sitcoms and the evening news play the game of life. The lines between what's a foul and what's in bounds, what's a penalty and what's a legal play are way too blurred for me.

Sure, when you're watching the Chiefs play you can throw away all that I just said. But when I surf my remote control beyond the world of sports into the vast darkness of the rest of the TV universe, I come across more strange worlds than the Starship Enterprise.

I sure felt like I was on another planet the other day while I was watching one of those real-life courtroom TV shows. The trial was about a young woman taking her brother to court because he didn't spend enough time with her son. That's right, she was taking her brother to court, not the kid's father.

She told the judge that since the boy's father was out of the picture, it was her brother's moral responsibility to be a father figure for her son.

That seemed foreign to me. I remember my mother never had to take my Uncle Charles "Peewee" Weston or any of my other uncles to court. Whether from a moral sense of duty or a sense of family, they all spent time being a father figure for me when I had no father.

Like I have said before, I was raised in a home where my grandmother wore the pants and my mother wore the belt out on me. Before she met my stepfather, my mother was a single mother for many years. And even though she and my grandmother were as strong as some men, they still couldn't provide a male role model for me.

My Uncle Pee-Wee died last Wednesday, and I'll always remember the date. It was November 22, the same day that two of my other people died. Former President John F. Kennedy and Christian apologist C.S. Lewis both died on that day in 1963.

Uncle PeeWee played a bigger role in my life than both men. For one thing, he bought me my first car.

The car surely was nothing special by today's standards or even that day's standards, for that matter. It was a black and white 1962 Chevy Impala that leaned to one side and never ran on all of its six cylinders at the same time. But it was mine and my uncle had given it to me and that was as special as it had to be.

My Uncle PeeWee taught me how to change the oil and the spark plugs and what each sound the car made meant.

Whenever the car would break down, which was often, it wouldn't matter where I was or what time of day or night, I could call him and he'd come get me started again. He never complained or grumbled about it either. He just showed me what was wrong so the next time I could fix it myself.

He also took the time to show me a lot of things about life and how to be a man. He taught me a lot about family responsibility.

When I got older, there were still nephews, nieces and cousins in our family that were being raised by single mothers. I figured I could do no less than what my Uncle PeeWee and other uncles had done for me through me childhood years. I figured it was my duty to try and provide some male support for them just like it was provided for me years ago.

The judge on that courtroom TV show didn't really rule in favor of the mother or her brother. He just said that if the brother was still living in the home he had some family responsibility. He told the woman that she couldn't force her brother to be someone he wasn't capable of being.

Not everyone can be like my Uncle PeeWee.

Memorial Day memories

Many of the pictures of Weston family get-togethers from long ago are kept in a huge photo book in my mother's attic.

The black-and-white photos are old, faded and crinkled now. Only the family members who were there then can make out the names of all the smiling faces behind the picnic table full of fried chicken, potato salad and cobblers.

But the images of those same reunion and family get-togethers seem to get brighter in my mind as the years go by.

I can close my eyes and see my aunt Bobbie trying to juggle one of my newborn cousins and a plate of potato salad on her lap like it was just yesterday.

I can still hear my Uncle Charley, whom everyone called Peewee because he was so small when he was born that they fed him out of an eyedropper, trying to play Elvis tunes on his guitar. I can still feel my Grandmother Lena looking over all of us grandkids to see how much we had grown since the last time.

She'd always check to see if we combed our hair. She'd do it herself if we didn't do it good enough to suit her. If she thought we were too skinny, she'd fix us another plate. I have to kneel at my grandmother's grave to let her look me over now.

I go to the cemetery on Memorial Day to visit her and the rest of the family I haven't seen in a while. It's a family reunion where no one remembers to bring the potato salad, but no one forgets the memories. As I walk among the graves of friends who died too young and family members who don't seem like they've been gone that long. It somehow grounds me. Perhaps more than anyone, these people know where I come from. To them, I'm just who I was when they last saw me. That image won't change for all eternity.

To many of them I'm Lonnie instead of Alonzo. I'm Tisie's only son. And, I'm still that skinny, nappy-headed kid who stuttered real bad and could read books and draw pictures all day if you'd let him. And I remember them all when they were at their best at being themselves. I see my Uncle Peewee not as he left, tied to a hospital bed with tubes coming from everywhere. I see him as a young man full of fast cars, guitars and Elvis.

I see my grandmother cooking Sunday dinner in the kitchen or walking home from the bus stop after working the snack bar at Katz Drug Store all day.

I see my childhood friend Lawrence Howard not like they all said he was after the car wreck, but swimming faster than everybody in the swimming pool at the old YMCA.

I see Linda Hedge, another childhood friend who died too young, walk across the stage as the queen in our fifth-grade Horace Mann school play.

I let them all look me over as I tell them about the new grandbaby, and how the wife and kids are doing. I hope I haven't disappointed any of them even if I do shave my head now. I go to the cemetery on Memorial Day like I go to the photo book in my mother's attic. It helps me remember.

Sometimes we learn the hard way from childhood's foolish stunts

Practically everyone has a vivid memory from the fourth of July from his or her childhood. For some, it's a family picnic. For others, it may be remembering the fireworks display. But for me, it's my grandmother yelling, "Lonnie, quit acting like such a gol darn fool!"

Now, taken out of context that statement would seem emotionally abusive. In these times, in which no one seems to take any blame for his or her actions, I could use it to explain much of my weird and demented behavior.

But the truth is, I was foolish around fireworks as a kid.

I did a lot of dumb things with them, like catching our roof on fire a few times and almost falling in the lake one year. I now suspect that's the reason every firework, except those little baby sparklers and smoke bombs, are illegal within the city limits today. It was because of dumb and foolish kids like me, years ago, blowing off fingers and burning up stuff. That's not to say there aren't kids who are foolish around fireworks today, because there are. But, if any adult is honest, he or she will readily admit that foolish firework behavior didn't start with this generation. We can't blame this one on MTV or Freddie Kruger.

Actually, I wasn't just foolish around fireworks and the Fourth of July. Throughout my childhood, I gave my grandmother plenty of reason to yell at me at other times during the year. Especially when I was about 12 years old. That was my glory year of foolish behavior, and I remember one incident in particular.

It was during this time in my life when I was pretty heavy into Spider-man and other comic book heroes. I was constantly reading about men flying and jumping off rooftops and out of windows, and I wanted to get in on that action.

I remember the roof on the next-door neighbor's house was so close to my upstairs bedroom that I became obsessed with jumping onto it. What added to the obsession was the fact that I could easily climb into the neighbor girl's bedroom window from the roof. Now, this girl paid me no attention at all, so why I wanted to risk swinging into her bedroom window is beyond me. But in my comic book-addled brain, I thought that if I just jumped on her roof one night and swung into her bedroom window, she would be so impressed that she would fall in love with me happily ever after.

I talked my friend Doug Vaughn into doing a trial run, one afternoon when the neighbors were out. I figured that if he didn't make it, I would forget the whole idea.

Doug sprung from my bedroom window and onto the neighbor's roof as easily and as fluidly as if Batman himself had done it. Now, I figured that since I was the better athlete, or so I thought, that it would be a piece of cake.

I got out on the windowsill. The Spider-man theme song began to play inside my head. I jumped.

Do you remember how in the cartoons, a character can walk on air for a while until he realizes that he's airborne and then falls straight down to the ground? Well I got out there in that space between my bedroom window and the neighbor's roof and froze in mid-flight. I quickly turned around in time to grab onto my bedroom windowsill. My feet swung from the momentum, not into the neighbor girl's open bedroom window, but into our closed, downstairs dining room window.

When I broke through the glass, it was my grandmother that was standing on the other side.

"Lonnie, quit acting like such a gol darn fool!"

I've gotten over my urge to jump out of windows since then. I don't play with fireworks much either.

Thanksgiving holds special meaning for family gatherings

When I look at pictures of Thanksgiving past, I see faces that are no longer at the table. And that is why I try to make sure I'm here at my mom's dinner table every year now, no matter how late the table is set.

For a few years, my wife and I would go to a restaurant for Thanksgiving dinner. We wanted to eat early and dinner at my mom's house was always late on Thanksgiving. It's funny how that never bothered me as kid.

I would wake up early Thanksgiving morning to the sounds of my grandmother Lena and mother in the kitchen making dressing and pies and washing collard greens. The smells of turkey and fresh bread would slowly begin to creep in from the kitchen to the living room where I sat watching Macy's Thanksgiving Day Parade.

Friends and relatives would creep in and out throughout the day. An aunt or two would come by to help out in the kitchen. A cousin, uncle or friend would drop by to check the score of the football games. Everybody would try to steal a fresh-baked roll before being chased out of the kitchen.

It would be those things like visitors, a stolen roll and a lick of a spoon that would tide us over while the meal was being prepared. It made the waiting fun. The stomachs growling in anticipation of the Thanksgiving meal would rival that of the sleepless night of Christmas Eve.

By the time the meal was finally done, it was usually dark outside. The house would be full of friends and family from out of town and around the neighborhood. It seemed like everyone would come to our green-shingled, two-story house on 16th Street. They called it 'going to Mama Lena's.'

They came to eat and tell stories and laugh. They came to show off new babies, new husbands, new wives, new cars, and new jobs. They came to talk about who was sick, who had got divorced, and who had died.

They were all family even if some of them you hated to see coming through the door.

And every Thanksgiving dinner had a least one person who wasn't there physically but who was there as part of the dinner conversation. They would die, leave town and/or leave the family. Every year one less plate would be fixed. One less turkey wing, drumstick or piece of pie would be wrapped in aluminum foil and put back for somebody. One less car would be parked in the yard or in front of the house. And every year we all became less and less patient about waiting on dinner.

We had microwaves, fast food and fast cars now and we didn't have to wait on anything—except in line for a bucket of chicken or a take-out meal.

The old house on 16th Street has been torn down quite sometime now. My grandmother died years ago and so have a few aunts, uncles, cousins and friends.

We have dinner at my mother and father's house now but I'll still catch myself looking around the dinner table to see whose plate is missing. Whether in memory of past guests or in anticipation of new ones, I know my folks will set out a few extra chairs anyways.

I may have to wait on dinner again tomorrow but time has taught me that I shouldn't miss it, even though I know I can eat three hours earlier in a restaurant somewhere with strangers.

Thanksgiving is about family and friends and it's with family and friends I want to be on Thanksgiving.

Taketh away is a reality we all have to have at some time

"The Lord giveth and the Lord taketh away."

I've heard that all my life. I've heard it at funerals, in sermons and in pool halls. I've heard it from old men who just gambled away their paychecks. And I've heard it several times from my grandmother's lips for several different reasons.

By hearing it and by saying it, it made losing something so much easier to take. You could blame it all on God's will and not your own.

"The Lord giveth and the Lord taketh away."

The passage just sounds like it comes from the Bible but I've never seen it there. It's just another one of those phrases like "The Lord helps those who help themselves" that sound so good that people hand it down through the years.

Now if that last phrase were actually in the Bible, we'd all be in trouble. That would mean we'd all have to meet the Lord halfway and even the most properly dressed Christian couldn't do that.

But "the Lord giveth and the Lord taketh away" could very well be in the Bible. It's a Biblical truth. And it's a truth that, sooner or later, rings bright in everyone's life.

That verity rings the loudest to me at Thanksgiving.

Between the turkey and the football is a time of reflection of what I have in my life at this particular time.

When I was a child, I honestly believed that my grandmother would always prepare Thanksgiving in our house at 314 S. 16th St. I couldn't imagine it any other way. I just knew the smell of turkey, greens, chitterlings, and cornbread would wake me up early Thanksgiving morning in time to watch the Macy's parade. I knew the Cowboys and the Lions would play later that day. And I knew our house would be full

15

of aunts, uncles and cousins laughing, talking and eating the day away.

But "the Lord giveth and the Lord taketh away." Through the years. things change. Those familiar smells of what grandmother was cooking in the kitchen no longer permeate the house. A few of the familiar faces no longer showed up. You begin to realize with each passing year some little bit of what you had the year before is now gone. You've taken them for granted for so long, it's only when they're gone that you realize with each passing year some little bit of what you had the year before is now gone. You've taken them for granted for so long, it's only when they're gone that you realize you should've given thanks for them while you had them.

But through the years the Lord still giveth. He replaced some of those people and those days with new people and new days and new things to be thankful for.

You may hate your job but next year you might not have a job. You may think your car is a piece of junk but next year you may not have any means of transportation. You may hate getting up in the morning to go to work but next year you may be too ill to work.

It would be nice if all the grudges, all the resentments and all the petty disagreements (let's face it, most are petty) were allowed to go on only for a year at the most. They should all have to be dropped by Thanksgiving. That would make it easier to tally up our blessings and not miss anyone or any- thing that we might not realize was a blessing if we didn't.

All of us, no matter how much we don't have, still have too much to be thankful for. We have to remember whomever or whatever it is, it could be gone next year.

"The Lord giveth and the Lord taketh away."

Silver aluminum Christmas trees vital part of family memories

When color TV's first came out, we naturally couldn't afford one. We barely kept our Motorola console, with spindly legs and a 15-inch screen, working to watch the "Ed Sullivan Show" on Sunday evenings. We wrapped aluminum foil on the rabbit ears. And all of us had to sit very still, so not to knock out the reception.

But, that never stopped my grandmother, Mama Lena.

She bought this colored plastic sheet from Katz Drug Store that was supposed to turn black and white sets into color ones, just by taping it to the screen. The sheet was tinted blue on top for sky, pink in the middle for skin tones, and green on the bottom third for grass. Sure, it wasn't a real color TV. We had to use our imagination, when the show moved indoors.

The same with landscaping. We could never afford shrubs, flowers, or cement statuary. That didn't stop Mama Lena. As long as Katz had discount and layaway, we wouldn't do without anything.

She would put these plastic ducks, swans, frogs, and all other types of low-priced landscaping on layaway in January and get it all out in time to plant in our yard by spring. I can laugh about that stuff today. But in my heart, I know that my grandmother tried to give us the best she could afford, even if it is tacky by today's standards.

That's why my nostalgia may by a little different than everyone else's. When most folks get sentimental for an old-fashioned Christmas, they usually long for a fresh-cut pine tree. But nothing gets me all misty-eyed and frog-voiced over Christmas past like one of those aluminum trees.

Whenever I look at old Christmas photos, the silver tree is always there like one of the family. It's like looking at a picture of a deceased relative or long-ago friend whom we never see anymore. With its many shimmering stalks of aluminum.

Del Wilson had two loves

The first time I shook hands with Adelbert "Del" Wilson was through a pickup window on a gravel road outside the Hemple General Store. That was about 20 years ago. His son and my friend, Rhys Wilson, introduced us.

Del's firm handshake and genuine smile told me I was meeting a good man.

Under a Stetson, Del looked like an old country-western singer or TV cowboy from the 1950s. Born in Billings, Montana and raised on a Manhattan, Kansas ranch, he had a Missouri twang that sounded just like a cowboy song.

And that's who Del Wilson was. A rodeo cowboy. An old cowboy still roping at 89 years old. He rode horses with his friends George Duncan, Larry Hirtler, Rusty Mooney and Terry Cotton up until he died.

Del Wilson died last week at the age of 90. You could say he died because he couldn't rope and ride like he wanted to anymore. For a man who lived for the sport, that could very well be true.

Or it could be all the bucking bronco busting and roping just wore out all his parts.

"He just got old on us," Rhys said.

Del was 82 when I saw him roping calves down at George Duncan's ranch in Taos. Moving as nimbly as a man half his age, he mounted his horse and shot out of the chute with lasso whirring, and roped the calf before it got halfway across the arena—a skill he learned as a young ranch hand when he moved back to Montana after serving in the Navy during World War II.

The skill got him a job as a commission man at the St. Joseph stockyards in 1952. He married the love of his life, Marjorie Rezac, a year later.

They celebrated their 60th anniversary earlier this year. Their last together. It's been a week since Del died and Marjorie hasn't got the hang of it yet of how to live life without him.

"She's trying to get over a habit she's had for 60 years," Rhys said.

Marjorie kept a bowl of stemmed grapes by Del's chair. She caught herself going to stem a bowl of grapes for him the other day.

"I think I did wait on him quite a bit. I start to do something and I think, I don't have to do it anymore," she said.

Del's cowboy hats still hang on a rack on the living room wall. It's still too early to take them down. His size 8 cowboy boots still sit underneath the living room bureau.

"Those were his marrying and burying boots. He wore them to funerals and weddings," Marjorie said.

Del was buried in the boots he wore. They put the last rope he used in the casket with him, too. His pocketknife, still sharp enough to cut off rope or a finger, was placed in his pocket.

Marjorie bought Del enough western string ties over the years to have enough for every son, grandson and great-grandson to wear at his funeral last Friday.

"There were about 20 or 25 of them in a box in the closet," she said.

The family found a book Rhys had given his dad about 10 years ago. It's called "A Father's Legacy." The book has pages a child might ask a father about and a place for the father to fill in the blanks.

Rhys read some of his dad's answers during the funeral.

When asked what was his favorite sport, everyone knew the answer.

"Being ranch raised, I guess rodeo," he wrote.

When asked about his most memorable Valentine's Day, Del scribbled a ready answer for that, too.

"I would have to say my most memorable one was a belated one. I got a wife on Feb. 19," he wrote.

Blessed is the man who has one love in his life. Del Wilson had two.

So long, old friend

Love strong

Bill and Velma Jean Hayden should have been celebrating their 50th wedding anniversary on January 3rd. The day found Bill making funeral arrangements for his wife of 50 years instead.

Velma Hayden died at 6:30 a.m. Friday. For two years, she fought death hard. In the hearts and minds of those who love her, death still didn't win.

On Christmas day, I wrote a column about Bill and Velma and how the St. Joseph couple dealt with her battles with bone cancer and the fact that Bill had lost his job recently. For Bill and Velma, the gift they wanted most was for her to be able to spend the holiday at home. They both spent Thanksgiving in the hospital cancer ward.

Bill and Velma brought in the New Year dealing with pain. She fought the hurt from the morphine needles in her back and the unbearable discomfort in her stomach. He tried coping with the fear of being alone.

"I'm tough, but I'm not that tough," Bill told me at Velma's wake Sunday evening. Bill still had a smile on Sunday. I probably wouldn't have recognized him if he didn't have one. For as long as I've known him, he's always had one handy. Smiles might be hard to come by for him now.

"It'll set in when I look over and not see her there in bed," he said.

What Bill said reminded me of "About Schmidt," a movie my wife and I saw over the weekend.

In the movie, Jack Nicholson portrays a recently retired man trying to make sense of his life. The character has a loving wife and daughter, a nice house and a financially secure bank account. It still wasn't enough to make him happy, though.

His daughter, an only child, was set to marry a guy he thought was a loser. He still loved his wife of 42 years but had started hating things about her, too.

It was the little things he hated. He hated the way she cut him off in conversation. He was repulsed by the way she walked. Even the way his wife smelled turned him off.

It was that same contempt of familiarity that sets in for many of us who are lucky enough to have someone around long enough to take them for granted.

Not trying to spoil the movie, but I have to tell you that the character's wife dies.

It isn't long afterward that he comes to realize how much of a hole she filled in his life.

It wasn't that he didn't know how to buy groceries or clean house. The bed was large and lonely now too. He even began to sniff his wife's perfume bottles because he missed her smell so much.

I reached for my wife's hand instead of the popcorn barrel this time. Sunday night, I held her tighter than usual as I thought of Bill, Velma and 50 years of loving the same person.

For us, it's over 20 years. Sometimes it seems longer, sometimes shorter but the love always comes out the same.

If you have someone to hug this morning, hold him or her tight. Hug your wife, hug your husband, hug your kids and call your parents often.

What little you think you may have today could be even less tomorrow. Let go of anger and resentment, but hold on tight to love, understanding and forgiveness.

Bill and Velma Jean held on to each other for 50 years. We're lucky to have anything that lasts that long.

The cherries came in season first.

The peaches came next, then the apricots, plums and tomatoes. Apples, pears and grapes came later.

No one told Larry Thomas and me that. We just knew whose yard had what tree or vine to raid. Larry and I ate our way through summer and fall out of other people's yards.

We sold pop bottles, threw newspapers, cut grass and cashed in store coupons for money.

The money went for soda pop, cupcakes, candy bars, comic books, footballs and basketballs. Larry and I went through about three footballs a year, stuffing them with rags when they got deflated until we could afford to buy another one.

That's what happens to footballs when you play with them in the street. Each dropped pass falls on asphalt, stripping away a little bit of pigskin each time.

You fall on asphalt, it strips part of your hide off, too. But that's how we played, hard and crazy. Football in the street under the streetlights. Fights underneath basketball rims hung to trees in alleys. We battled for rebounds on a court made of dust and gravel, each of us, depending on the season, imitating a different sports hero.

During football season, Larry was Gale Sayers, I was Bob Hayes. In basketball, I was Oscar Robertson and he was John Havlicek. In baseball, we were anybody who happened to be hot with a bat or on the mound at the time. In 1968, we both were Bob Gibson.

Larry's baby sister, Diane, sent me a text last week. She was just a baby when Larry and I were in our childhood adventures but she knew we were old friends. Diane, or Dee Dee, wanted me to know before I heard it on the street. Police found Larry dead in an apartment in Portland. He was planning to move back to Kansas City but went back to Portland for a few days. He had been living there.

All the childhood memories you thought you forgot come back clear when a childhood friend dies. The milestones and trials of adulthood and everyday life can drown them out sometimes. Raising kids, taking care of bills and your job leave little time for that reflection sometimes.

But it is refreshing and a tonic to the soul to look back to those days and see what struggles and joys you had then. They were simpler and purer somehow. Everything was an adventure.

Lover's Lane is a long walk from 16th and Charles for a kid. Larry and I made that walk to get money from a guy who owed us for cutting grass. Poor kids on a journey through a rich neighborhood to confront a rich man who owed us money. Larry and I did that.

Larry and I egged the windows of a North End laundromat one time because a woman who worked there was rude to us. Cops took us home. At home, we got in more trouble for wasting groceries. You don't fight with food, you fight over it.

I make enough money now to buy cases of bottled water. None of it tastes as good as it did from a garden hose after a pickup baseball game. No apple tastes better than one stolen from a neighbor's tree. No girl was prettier than the one you dreamed about. And we dreamed about many.

I'd lost track of Larry in later years. The last time I saw him was in the late 1980s. Always a gentle soul, unless in a pickup basketball game; he was a young man then, still seeking spirituality. I apologized again for the permanent scar I made on his forehead from a fight we had during a game. It bothers me now that he died with that scar. The memory of how he got it never died. The only fight we ever had over a stupid sandlot game we both long forgot.

25

What I'll remember about Larry Thomas is that he made my childhood richer just by knowing him.

So long, my friend. We'll eat stolen apples again together someday.

The face on the jar

A pack of cigarettes and a bag of chips pretty much empty out a $5 bill. Yet the young man scooped up the remaining change and without much thought dropped it in the large pickle jar at the end of the convenience store counter.

A small matter for most people. But you notice things like that if you know the face on the jar.

I knew Andy (not his real name). But I hadn't seen my childhood friend for years until now. And now I see his much-older face photocopied and taped to a pickle jar sitting on a convenience store counter. The crude script below his fading picture says something about his family needing help.

That jogged my memory a little. I remembered that Andy died a few weeks back.

He was the same age as me.

He was the same guy who, when we were kids, liked to spread his whole comic book collection out on the front lawn. He didn't collect them. He just liked to look at them. He read them and traded them off for ones he didn't own.

I remember when Andy and I would read comic books on his front porch until the cicadas came out. Sometimes we'd read by flashlight.

Some days Andy and I would come home sweaty, thirsty and covered in mud.

We were survivors from the dirt clod wars up on Devil's Backbone. We'd wash our faces and hands and drink from the garden hose on the side of his house and go inside for a glass of Kool-Aid and a bologna sandwich with cheese.

We'd stack pop bottles at Jake's Drug Store for spending money. But we'd always give it right back. The money we earned bought us more comic books, soda pop and cupcakes. Money really could buy happiness then.

Andy and I rode our bicycles all over town. Dogs chased us and barked at the playing cards thrashing against our spokes. We played chicken, daring each other to do something dumber and more dangerous each time. It had to be something dumb enough to make us both laugh.

Still waiting in line, I occupy my thoughts by staring at the face on the jar.

Somehow I can't believe it was the same kid. But I knew. Even though I hadn't seen Andy for years, I knew.

Maybe I didn't recognize some of the lines on his face. I wasn't there when he got them. He probably wouldn't recognize the lines on my face either. They're some touches we've both added, such as wives, children and grandchildren, in the years since we've lost touch.

Even behind the tattered wear and paper smudges, Andy's eyes looked more tired than I remembered. They looked as if they'd seen twice the years listed on his birth certificate. At some point, they had captured pain and never got around to letting it go.

Everyone in line before me put change in the jar. A few pennies, a dime, a quarter, a wadded up dollar bill. Their generosity covered the bottom of the jar.

I didn't ask any of them if they knew Andy. I figured it wouldn't matter anyway.

And if they did know him, I figured my asking would embarrass them somehow into thinking I was checking how much they put in the jar.

Really it didn't matter how much money any of us put in the jar. It would never have seemed like enough.

Lost too soon

To sleep well at night is a blessing. A good night's sleep is a gift many of us take for granted.

Sometimes an illness or physical aches and pains rob us of our slumber. It keeps us awake by reminding us of our ailments. But a pain pill or a stiff drink usually helps us forget.

After we get past the physical, it comes down to the mental. What troubles us during the day sometimes haunts our nights. How well did we do? Did we do the best we could? Were we nice to others? Were we nice to ourselves?

After we tally all those things up, it comes down to our family and friends. One by one we check them off. Thanking God for the ones who are doing OK. Praying for the ones who aren't. And hoping we wind up with more thanks than requests.

When one of your family or friends is hurting, sleep feels like a guilty pleasure.

What for you is a given, is for them a treasure. You have so much of what they have so little. All you can share is their pain.

The past several nights have been hard for me to sleep because I knew that two of my dearest friends couldn't.

Mike McCann and Joyce Humel lost their youngest son, Alex Humel McCann, last Friday.

He was 17. Alex, who suffered from epilepsy, died in his sleep.

Alex was a worldly young man. He had an emotional maturity and wisdom that extended beyond his teen years. No doubt much of that maturity came from having good parents.

Mike and Joyce value people. And they value experiences over material things.

They made sure their sons had plenty of experiences and valued other people.

But some of Alex's maturity has to be attributed to the fact that in his short 17 years, he experienced more than many of us will in a lifetime.

He spent part of his childhood growing up in the poorest regions of Botswana, Africa. No TV. No video games. No electricity. Just books and heart.

Mike and Joyce quit their good jobs here and went to Africa in 1994 to do mission work. They took Alex and his older brother, Nick, along with them.

Alex was well traveled. Besides living for a time in Africa, he visited 22 countries in his 17 years. And he was passionate, not just about the usual things a 17-year-old boy is passionate about like cars and girls, but about humanity. Alex would travel anywhere to support causes for peace and justice.

He cared. He was genuine.

I first met Alex after I started working at the News-Press 16 years ago. Mike was a region reporter here at the time and we quickly became friends.

I got to know Joyce through Mike and also through serving on the Rolling Hills Regional Library board. At the time Joyce was assistant director of the Rolling Hills Regional Library.

We too became good friends, and Alex became my favorite.

Mike used to have a photo of Alex on his desk when he worked here at the paper.

Alex was about 4 years old in the picture. And in the photo he looked like some latter-day Dickens character, wearing a railroader's hat and jacket. He also wore this determined look on his face.

I liked the photo so much that Mike made me a copy. And for a long while it sat on my desk too, and after that on my living room bookcase at home.

I watched Alex grow through the years. I saw him get taller. I heard his voice get deeper. I saw he could grow a full beard at 16. But that look in his eyes never changed. Not even the last time I saw him.

A few weeks ago, my wife and I went to visit Mike and Joyce in their Lakewood, Ohio, home. It was a great visit. We did lots of things. Mike, Joyce and Alex were great hosts. We went to a Cleveland Cavaliers game, the Rock and Roll Hall of Fame, the Football Hall of Fame and attended a gospel brunch at the House of Blues.

But of all those things, one part of our visit sticks out above them all. Especially now.

Mike, Joyce, Deanna and I had plans to go out to a jazz club one evening. But Alex insisted we stay in and have a home-cooked dinner instead. He just wanted to visit.

Joyce had bought Mike some cooking lessons from some well- known chef as a gift earlier. And he used that gift to whip us up a very good meal.

But Alex wanted the night to be really special. He turned down the lights, brought out the candles and put some real good jazz on the stereo. He then sat down next to me and asked that we all hold hands and say grace. That's how Alex was. Thoughtful. Compassionate. Full of grace and genuine. And that's what I'll remember to help me sleep at night.

Mom is finally moving

When Dad died four years ago, Mom said she'd never move from the house. It was their home, bought and paid for with wages from working the hot-dog line at Seitz and the cash register and snack bar at Osco Drugs.

For me, it was Mom and Dad's house; for my kids, it was Grandma and Grandpa's house; and for everyone else, it was Tootlebug and Tisie's house—Henry and Florestine Turner's nicknames since childhood. A childhood they shared as next-door neighbors. Sweethearts since their teens, when Pop would buy Mom chocolate malts and Juicy Fruit gum from behind the counter at Ozenberger's Ice Cream parlor where he worked as a soda jerk.

Mom's ready to move now. This place began to feel even bigger with Pop gone. She and I talked about her childhood, memories made in this house and other things, as she got ready to move to a smaller place.

Everything she packed away jostles a memory. Sixty-plus years of stories, packed away in cardboard boxes. Photos of long-gone relatives, and of Christmas parties, Thanksgiving dinners and Easter suits.

Mom still has kept my baby shoes, the pictures I drew for her as a kid and almost every newspaper article I've ever written stuffed in drawers and closets. She even has the one-piece jumpsuit I wore back in the disco days. That's one piece of nostalgia you can bet gets thrown away.

Whenever you move, you dismantle history and take it with you. You pack as many of the memories made in the place you're leaving to use as seeds for the memories you'll make in the new place.

But some memories you'll leave behind. They forever stay with the house.

The memories of Pop playing the organ and singing at Christmas stays in the house on Sylvanie. It's one of the few times anything took place in the living room, which was reserved for holiday celebrations and serious family discussions. Those things Mom and Pop felt required using the best furniture in the house. And an organ.

I can't remember the last time Pop carved the turkey and said grace on Thanksgiving in the dining room. I know the dinner guests changed through the years. Plates with no food on them still got set.

Mom's good dinner plates now gather dust in the china cabinet. Those dinners take place at our house now. But it's not the same. Never will be.

No longer will I see Mom in this kitchen, frying chicken and baking pies. The smells from the kitchen linger only in memory here. In the new place, they'll move.

We say goodbye to the oak tree in the backyard, where Pop and my son sat and drank sweet tea after cutting the grass.

We say goodbye to the prettiest lawn on the block when Pop was alive. The Christmas decorations that covered the yard and brightened the neighborhood every year sit in the basement now until someone sees a need for them again.

I'll miss seeing Mom sitting up high in her porch rocker, looking out over the neighborhood, complaining about the cats and the cars that speed up and down Sylvanie Street. She'll still wonder if the little dog across the street will get run over or not. That's just Mom.

She didn't sleep on her last night in the old house. Mom stayed up all night packing, she said. I believe she didn't want to spend her last night in the home asleep. She wanted to savor every last moment awake. Let the wee hours of morning conjure up more memories. Maybe in that half-asleep, half-awake state it would all seem like a dream.

She could say goodbye tomorrow.

Marriage vows come years after relationship is built

Although I just celebrated my two-year wedding anniversary last week, it felt like it was my sixteenth.

Wait a minute. Let me clarify that statement lest my wife, Deanna, sees to it that this will be the last column I write. Or the last breath I take, for that matter.

You see, before we got married a couple of years ago, we lived together for 14 years. That's right, 14 years.

It's not so strange, actually. A lot of people live together for years and, for whatever reason, never get married. Take my mom and dad. They've been together for more than 20 years and still haven't married. By all accounts, they are married: they act like they're married and they get along better than anyone I know—or so it seems.

I'm in no way condoning cohabitation. Heaven forbid. Every right-winger in the country will heap wrath upon me.

The reason Deanne and I waited so long to get married didn't have anything to do with experimenting with cohabitation or trying to break my parent's record.

I'd already been through one divorce, and she'd seen her parents go through many, so we both agreed to work out personal problems before we got married so our marriage wouldn't turn out that way. We wanted to wait for the perfect time to get married. Actually that was one of the few things we agreed upon during those 14 years.

We weren't really compatible. She's numbers. I'm words. She thinks linear. I think abstract. I like old movies, and she likes new movies... I'd better stop here before this turns into a commercial for cigarettes. You get the picture.

But we weren't always at different ends of the spectrum. We both liked sports, music and many other things. She was like a running buddy as well as a lover. She still is.

But we fought. We made mistakes. We thought each year that the next one would be when we'd have it all worked out. But each year came and went and it still wasn't the right time.

Do you ever try hard to do something for so long, like learning to ride a bike and having sex, and suddenly in the trying you're doing it?

That's the realization Deanna and I came to a couple years ago. Despite our problems, mistakes and differences we still hung together and worked through them. Our relationship was working and it took us 14 years to realize it.

We still make mistakes. We still argue about the kids and the remote control. She still likes soul music and Mexican food and I still like jazz and barbecue. There're new problems everyday, and we get stronger everyday.

I believe there is never a perfect time for marriage.

There is never a time when the stars are just right or one day you both wake up and get along forever and ever.

Marriage isn't some pinnacle to reach and once you get there you can rest on your laurels. It is a forever-ascending mountain that we must continue to climb.

I've been married 16 years and I hope many more to come. Happy Anniversary, Deanna. Love, Alonzo.

It's been several years since I'd seen Dr. DuMont.

That's why I didn't know what to expect when I knocked on his door in Country Squire Residence retirement village Tuesday morning.

The door itself gave nothing away. Just a gold plate like they issued to everyone in the village, only this one had the name Clement C. DuMont engraved in it. The fall decoration on his door was probably a retirement village idea too. I couldn't imagine Dr. DuMont being concerned with such things.

For close to 40 years, Dr. DuMont was the doctor for the people in St. Joseph. He never turned anyone away. He was always accessible. And he lived right in the neighborhood, not in some fancy housing addition far, far away from his patients. You could always knock on his door or call him on the phone and he would answer. He was concise in both life and word, never saying more than needed to be said.

Dr. DuMont delivered both my children during a time when fathers weren't allowed in the delivery room.

I remember waiting impatiently outside the delivery room door while my son was being born, waiting for Dr. DuMont to finally come out. I wasn't sure what I expected him to say, maybe tell me how fat the baby was or if he or she had hair. But all he said was, "You have a boy." And with that, he walked away, off to his daily rounds. Sure it wasn't much, but it told me all I needed to know and that my boy was healthy.

When you went to his office, Dr. DuMont was just as concise. It was usually just "You have a cold," or "You have strep throat." And if he could cure what ailed you without medication, he'd do it.

I remember as a kid going to him for a bad case of warts on my fingers. Instead of prescribing medication, Dr. DuMont simply told me to put adhesive tape on the warts at night and pull the tape off in the morning. The tape eroded the warts away.

"Come in!" said a voice from behind the door, jarring me from my memories. It was a familiar voice that wavered a little since the last time I heard it. But it was still as direct as I remembered it.

Dr. DuMont looked tall even sitting in his recliner. A thin blanket barely covered his 6-foot, 3-inch frame while he watched television. He reads more than he watches and he doesn't watch much TV.

"The History Channel, National Geographic, Discovery and the news," he said.

As if providing proof, roughly two months' worth of newspapers lay on the floor beneath an end table decorated with a magnetic sticker of the Canadian flag. A simple reminder of his native British Columbia.

The rest of Dr. DuMont's apartment had no more furniture or accessories than needed. Nice, clean, unassuming and functional, just like the Midtown he once lived in. Just like him.

"I was never fond of fancy things," he said.

What did surprise me was a can of Copenhagen sitting on the table. When I saw it, a fleeting image of those old doctor-endorsed cigarette ads from the 1950s flashed through my mind.

"I chewed tobacco for 75 years. But you can count my fingers to tell how many cigarettes I've smoked," Dr. DuMont said, smiling and holding up 10 long digits from a pair of still steady hands. Those were the hands that brought more than 6,000 babies into the world, from a medical career that spanned from 1948 to 1985. Many of them came in for free.

"People had no money," Dr. DuMont said matter-of-factly.

Country Squire Residence will host a birthday open house from 2 to 4 p.m. this Saturday to celebrate Dr. DuMont's 90th birthday. It would be nice if 6,000 people showed up. After all, he showed up for their birthday. But if you'd ask Dr. DuMont he doesn't need all the fuss. Never has.

"I don't care if I'm remembered," he said. "I've just never been one for publicity."

OUR
ST.JOSEPH

Newspapers reveal history of black community

Newspapers reveal history one day at a time. It's our story told as it unfolds. One day our future generation will look back at today's news as a history lesson.

I don't know if newspapers will be around in 50, or even 25 years, but the news will still be vital to a well-informed society.

Looking back on old news as history gives us the advantage of knowing the past so we don't repeat the mistakes. It also reminds us that nothing is new. History often repeats itself.

Looking through old news clippings this past month provided a history lesson of little known facts about the St. Joseph black community.

It's easy to think blacks in St. Joseph during the late 1800s were paralyzed to the point of inaction and idleness by the racism and segregation that was written into law. In spite of those hindrances, I found a people with ambition, a belief in self and a strong sense of community.

A few random clippings from that time period, some ambitious, some humorous, show ways we've changed and some ways we haven't:

St. Joseph Daily Herald, Sept. 27, 1896: "The colored McKinley Club held a meeting last evening at the hall at Fifth and Felix streets, with over 100 members present." One of the guest speakers at the meeting was Isaiah Harris, an 85-year-old St. Joseph resident who was one of the first few blacks to vote in the city. He always voted the straight Republican ticket, according to the article. The first colored school was held inside his home.

St. Joseph Daily Gazette, Aug. 20, 1889: " Reverend W.W. Stewart, the colored Baptist minister who has been charged with being the father of the illegitimate child of a former member of his flock, returned to St. Joseph Sunday morning and was engaged up to last night in preparing a statement for the newspapers." The minister denied paternity, saying he took the Mary Jones out on buggy rides quite often, but that was it. He claimed the girl didn't really know the baby's father. Part of his defense as reported in the paper read: "He says one Washington saw Mary and a certain man in the wet of criminality and in consequence of the former's approach they were frightened away... Mr. Stewart also asserts that she had a hankering for the Dr. Middleton Indian Show, which held the boards in St. Joseph last summer."

St. Joseph Daily Gazette, Aug. 2, 1889: "Yesterday was the anniversary of the emancipation of slaves in the West Indies and the event was duly celebrated by the colored people of St. Joseph and surrounding cities at New Ulm Park."

St. Joseph Daily Gazette, Oct. 7, 1887: "Gabriel Scott, a colored man, who has been at the county poor farm for the past two months died on Monday last at the advanced age of 105 years... Scott was the oldest person in northwest Missouri with the exception of an old negro woman residing on Levee and Franklin streets known as 'Aunt Jenny' who is now past 108 years."

St. Joseph Daily Gazette, Oct. 30, 1888: "The Independent Colored Voters of St Joseph have organized themselves into a club with headquarters at No. 210 Francis Street."

St. Joseph Daily Gazette, Nov. 6, 1887: "The African M.E. Church people have erected a neat parsonage on their lot, corner Third and Antoine streets, at a cost of one thousand six hundred dollars and they take this method of reaching all friends who are willing to aid in paying off the debt. How much will you give?"

A proud history of schools

My kids were surprised when I first told them that for a time, I attended an all-black school.

Bartlett High School became Horace Mann Elementary School shortly after school integration. For the first four or five years of my schooling, I attended Horace Mann, which didn't become fully integrated until after school busing took place around 1967 or 1968.

Looking back, the experience wasn't much different than at any other school: The teachers and administration were all about educating children.

What was different was there was a little more emphasis on black history. Framed photos of Paul Lawrence Dunbar and Booker T. Washington hung on the walls alongside pictures of presidents.

The teachers and administrators also lived in the neighborhood. They taught our parents and relatives. It was schooling as community; the education extended beyond the walls of the school.

It was the leftover spirit from Bartlett High School. The main part of the school building was torn down, but the original Bartlett gym and stage area remain to this day to remind us.

Bartlett had its beginnings as the Colored High School. It was merely a rented room in a building on Frederick Avenue and 20th Street. It existed from 1885 to 1888 at that location before moving to 18th and Angelique streets and becoming the Colored High and Grammar School.

As an aside, the Colored State Teachers Association also met in St. Joseph at the Francis Street Baptist Church in 1888. School Superintendent E.B. Neely gave the welcoming address to a gathering of about 30 members of the association. Throughout the day, several educators and dignitaries gave speeches on the state of the black population in regard to education.

Professor G.M. Grisham of Kansas City spoke of the necessity of an education and how it would help solve many, if not all, of the problems of the negro race.

Association President R.T. Coles spoke about the responsibilities and burdens facing colored teachers. He said unlike in the white school where all the teachers had to do was teach, black teachers must not only teach, but be social leaders.

The Colored High and Grammar School opened on March 5, 1889, with 291 high school and elementary students and eight rooms. On March 7, students and community members gathered at the school as a Professor I.E. Page of Lincoln Institute in Jefferson City and Professor G.N. Grimshaw of Kansas City delivered speeches for the building dedication, according to the St. Joseph Daily Gazette.

On June 22 of that year, the first five students to graduate from the school—valedictorian Lillie Jackson, salutatorian Linnie Montgomery, Lesa Ross, Toni Cockrell and Katie Cunnigan—received their diplomas on stage inside the Tootle Opera House.

Newspaper accounts of the night described it as one given to excellent speeches and music, all done with an air of dignity.

"It was something of a novelty to see the curtain rise on five young colored women, elegantly and tastefully attired, dignified in bearing and impressed with the solemnity of the notable occasion," read one newspaper account of the event.

The Colored High and Grammar School was renamed Bartlett High School in 1904 in honor of the benefactors of the school, the Bartlett family.

Douglass School in the South Side and Lincoln School in the north part of town served black elementary school students.

Bartlett closed in 1954 after school integration and became Horace Mann School.

By most accounts, school integration didn't run into the dissension here as it did in other places. A big part of the reason was that while the schools were segregated, the neighborhoods for the most part were not. Black and white kids grew up as neighbors and played together. Going to school together wasn't a big deal.

The same was true for school busing, which was an attempt to further integrate the schools. I was part of that first class that went through busing at Horace Mann. Friendships were formed during that year that last to this day.

Rec center took decades to become reality

More than 200 people met inside the St. Francis Baptist Temple on an October Monday in 1928. Led by a group called the Young Negro Men's Progressive Club, the mission was to get the city to approve purchase of a building for a black community center.

Black St. Joseph residents at the time didn't have a place to hold large social functions or to provide recreational opportunities for its youth. The Young Negro Men's Progressive Club hoped the City Council would grant an ordinance to approve the purchase of a building at 19th and Messanie streets for those purposes.

A committee of about 20 members of the black community—ministers, school principals and representatives from the Negro YMCA and YWCA, along with members of the Young Negro Men's Progressive Club—presented the proposal to the city.

The location of the site was a huge concern. That concern caused the City Council to delay the purchase of the Messanie Street location for the center.

Ironically, the area around 19th and Messanie was considered a black neighborhood, with more than a few black businesses including the office of Dr. E.Y. Strawn, a black physician, at 1908 Messanie St.

But the area also had a substantial white community— many of the residents who lived in the area called Goosetown, which is roughly bounded by Sylvanie and Olive streets between 14th and 24th streets.

Opposition came from some residents around the Sts. Peter and Paul Church on Messanie and Warsaw Streets. Joseph E. Lorenz who lived at 505 S. 20th St. at the time served as spokesperson for the opposition on behalf of about 150 white residents who lived in the area.

He cited depreciation of white-owned property, residential district location, use of public money for one class of citizens and interracial contact as some of the main reasons for the opposition.

"We are not opposed to giving the Negroes fair treatment but we are emphatically opposed to having the community building placed in our neighborhood," Mr. Lorenz read from a statement to the council as reported in the St. Joseph Daily Gazette. He suggested sites around Fourth and Faraon streets, for the location of the community center.

Leon Stewart, secretary of the Negro YMCA, followed Mr. Lorenz's statements with a resolution signed by all the black churches, the black YMCA, black YWCA and other black organizations in the community.

"The negro citizens of St. Joseph are united in their request that the city select the 19th and Messanie site," he said. "It is in the heart of a negro community. There you will find our homes, our schools, our organizations and our community life," he said.

Further news reports showed the City Council failed to act on approval of the recreation center. Although the location for the proposed center was unclear, city directories from 1928 to 1930 show grocer O.P Henson, at 1901 Messanie, and another grocer, J.C. Borkowski, at 1902 Messanie, as possible sites.

That need would continue into the 1970s when efforts by another coalition of black community members called Black Citizens for Progress enlisted the help of the community to purchase an old grocery store at 20th and Messanie streets and turn it in a recreation center for black youth. That mission succeeded. A building was later constructed on the site and named the East Side Human Resource Center. The organization later moved to the 18th and Sylvanie streets location and became the Bartlett Center.

Any act of revisiting history shows that it often repeats it-self. That's why knowing what came before is so important.

When she found out

Theresa Rowlett was well into her 30s when she found out.

Her mother never told her. Friends and relatives didn't tell her either.

But Ms. Rowlett said a woman she worked with at Einbender's clothing store took her aside and told her about the 1933 St. Joseph lynching. She even showed her pictures.

"She said, Theresa, look at the way they tarred and feathered this man,'" Ms. Rowlett said Monday from her Midtown home. "That's how I found out. Then I asked my mama."

Only then did her mother bring out the painful old secret. Perhaps she had hoped the stories would die away before her kids found them. They didn't.

Folks say when they're old enough to ask, they're old enough to know. So the mother had the daughter pull up a chair.

She opened up the store of painful memories. Memories she'd kept locked up since that November night in 1933.

She let the frightening images tumble out: an angry white mob breaking into the city jail and dragging out a 19-year-old black man accused of assaulting a white woman; the mob kicking and stabbing the young man's body as they drug him to the corner of Fifth and Jules streets; images of how they hanged him and set his body on fire; and scenes of black people all over town hiding in fear of being lynched too.

"They were hiding under porches and everything. "Mama said they probably would have lynched us all if they would have found us,'" Ms. Rowlett said.

Then her mother told her. The man lynched that night was her uncle, Lloyd Warner. He had confessed to and later denied the crime. No one was ever convicted in his murder.

And that was why she never got to meet mom's brother. "That happened in '33 and I was born in '34," she said.

That's about 20 years before the Emmett Till murder in 1955. The Emmett Till case came to light again last week after the FBI said no federal charges would be filed in the brutal death of the 14-year-old black teen from Chicago.

Till was visiting relatives in Mississippi in 1955 when he was killed and thrown into the river for whistling at a white woman. An all-white jury acquitted the two men who later confessed to the murder.

Several books and documentaries have been made about the case.

The FBI decided not to file charges because of the time issue. Federal charges for civil rights' crimes carry a five-year statue of limitations. That now leaves it up to the state of Mississippi to seek charges in the boy's death.

"It's up to [District Attorney Joyce L. Chiles] now and the state of Mississippi that's been given a rare chance to redeem themselves," said Emmett Till's cousin, Simeon Wright, in an Associated Press interview. "They claim that they have changed. We're going to see."

Ms. Rowlett has seen many things change in 70-plus years. But she said she's never seen much reason to revive old hurts. People don't want to hear about them anyway.

"That's bygones. I didn't know him," she said. "Some folks are going to say, why are you bringing up that old stuff?' That's old stuff, but still."

I asked Ms. Rowlett if she would welcome the idea of receiving an apology from the city for the murder of her uncle. After all, he was in city custody at the time of his death.

She gave an answer that pretty much said she learned long ago not to wait around for apologies. If you do, you might be standing still most of the time.

"Do you think we'll get one?" she asked, as if already knowing the answer.

Black Archives looks to the past to aid the future

It took about a year for 1968 to reach St. Joseph. All the unrest, despair and anger brought about by the assassinations of Martin Luther King Jr. and Robert F. Kennedy and the Democratic National Convention fallout didn't really hit St. Joseph until 1969. Sure, we felt the pain from those events too, but local tragedy prompted the St. Joseph black community to say "enough is enough." The local anger and despair combined with the local angst to create a force for change. It also opened our eyes in some ways to see what all we lacked.

In the spring of 1969, a white police officer shot and killed Richard Marvin Ginn, a young black male, in an empty lot at 17th and Messanie streets.

The circumstances were dubious. Black residents demanded an inquest. The prosecutor denied it. Anger ensued.

Gary Wilkinson remembers the time well. "There was a lot of unrest at that time. Tension in the community was pretty high," he said. "Things started to hit home," Mr. Wilkinson added. "We had the different ideologies of how do we go about it? Martin Luther King was nonviolent, Malcolm X wanted to get it by any means necessary, and we had the Black Panthers coming out at that time. It was pretty exciting."

The unrest turned into action.

A group of young black forward-thinking residents formed the Black Contemporary Society. The group evolved into Black Citizens for Progress, Mr. Wilkinson said.

Much of the problem was the lack of a recreational outlet for black youths like Richard Marvin Ginn in the community. That became the goal.

"They came together, joined together with Joyce Raye Patterson from InterServ. She had a big role in getting things going," Mr. Wilkinson said. "Then they got some influential members of the white community involved in it—Bob Simpson, Jerry Maag, Milton Litvak—they came together and discussed it and finally came up with a plan: they wanted to develop a youth center."

Out of the plan came the East Side Human Resource Center, which became the current Bartlett Center.

"What I can see looking back at things that happened at the time, it was a really intense time, a lot of things going on. There was a war going on, (and) there's some parallels you can draw with the atmosphere today that young people are facing," Mr. Wilkinson said.

And police are killing black youths today.

"We have to look at what happened in the past to make sure it's not repeated. That's why it's good to look at history," Mr. Wilkinson said.

My 25 years as a reporter

A friend once told me that I should write a book about all the jobs I've had. I've probably worked more jobs than David Jansen did when he played "The Fugitive."

I sold vacuum cleaners, worked on the railroad, worked in a bakery, a grain mill, a chemical plant, made phone booths, paper boxes, cut grass, stacked pop bottles, threw papers, mopped floors, spooled wire and plowed snow off roadways.

I've left jobs in probably every way possible too. I've been fired (more than once), quit, was laid off, downsized, let go.

But no job I had ever really defined me. Of course, I took pride in my work as I always felt any honest job disgraces no man.

When I was a baker, I was a baker. When I was a wire rope man, I was a wire rope man. When I was a janitor, I was a janitor. I was all those things, but that's not who I felt I was inside.

I felt I was a writer but was too busy trying to make a living to pursue that career. The bills had to be paid.

Bill Guenther used to have a 24-hour gym on Eighth and Charles streets in the late 1970s. For almost two years, five nights a week, my routine was to walk there from work at the bakery on Frederick, go to the library and walk home. Each trip I would look over at the News-Press building and imagine working here. I would come in from time to time and ask about being a part-time reporter. Each time, I got turned down.

Someone, somewhere, knew I was not ready at that time. When the time was right, it would come.

On June 6, 1989, it did. The time was right. The managing editor Bob Waldrop gave me a three-month internship on the recommendation of Taju Tubbs, a local community activist and neighborhood friend. When Mr. Waldrop left, George Lockwood became managing editor. Through our love of jazz and comics, we became friends. He asked me to stay. At this time, I was still working at Wire Rope during the night and part time at the News-Press during the day.

I worked both jobs for 10 years—blue collar by night, white collar by day—until Bob Unger came along as managing editor and hired me full time.

A few weeks ago, I celebrated 25 years working for the News-Press. It's the longest I've been on any one job. And I can say there has never been a day go by when I did not love what I do.

In 25 years, I've seen tragedy and joy up close. I've interviewed mothers and fathers who have lost children to murder and car wrecks. I listened to old men tell tall tales around a pot-bellied stove in an old gas station.

I've been in most every small town in the area. What I've learned is we are all basically the same around here. We respect good manners and good people and a good home-cooked meal. We take pride in hard work and when there is a need, we come together.

I've interviewed farmers and farm wives, jazz musicians, politicians, athletes and authors. I interviewed men in suits and men in coveralls. I tromped through fields to get a story and got mud on my shoes. I got dust on my car from barreling down gravel roads to get to some small spot on the map.

I've seen monks cry, remembering their own who got killed. I've consoled a mother whose son, a war veteran, had taken his own life. I've seen tree-climbing dogs and museums in garages. I've been run out of places and threatened to be shot.

I would not trade any of it for a million dollars. I count it a blessing to see and understand the human condition in a way I never would have before. God knew when it was the right time for me to be here.

The time machine on my porch transports me to my idyllic youth

I have a time machine, and it's my front porch.

When I sit there on an evening, close my eyes and let my other senses take over, I can go anywhere. The cacophony of children's noises from the playground across the street, the birds in the trees, the barking dogs, the early summer breeze I feel, the smell of early blooms, and the hint of rain provide the fuel to transport me back to another time, another porch.

If I ride the wave of my senses long enough, I'm on the front porch at 314 S. 16th St., the address of my youth. The noises beget other noises. The smells bring to mind other smells long ago and, even though my eyes are closed, they peer through the years. The children's voices now belong to my childhood friends. I hear Doug Vaughn, Kenny McDonald and Larry Thomas bouncing a basketball down the street headed for my house for another pickup game. I see Billy Brandt and me playing with plastic army men in the Jolly Roger Ice Cream truck so plainly that I can see the red-and-white-striped behemoth of a truck and the dark-haired man in the white suit we knew only as the "Jolly Roger Man." I see the balloon man coming down the street with a bouquet of red, blue and yellow orbs and twirlybirds on sticks dancing around his silvery white head. The only feature you can make out is his bulbous red nose.

My eyes squint and my nose burns from the smell of the bug man's truck that shoots huge billows of kerosene-laden smoke designed to kill the mosquitoes on a hot summer night. I see kids from neighborhoods far away entangled in the strands of smoke running behind the truck, trying to keep up.

I see my grandmother coming down from the hill after the streetcar has let her off, and I can smell exhaust as it pulls away. I still breathe in the piquant scent of hamburgers and

French fries and bacon and eggs on her clothes from the short orders she prepared at the lunch counter all day at Katz Drug Store downtown.

The breeze somehow feels cooler, until I realize it's from the sweat that's evaporated on my T-shirt from playing a sand- lot football game on old man Thompson's lot. I can still taste lunchmeat and Kool-Aid, my supper because it's too hot to cook.

I hear the first few strains of Wagon Train coming through the wooden screen door on my porch. I don't have to see it. I know it comes from a black-and-white mahogany television set with spindly antelope legs and an identity complex that's personified by the tri-colored plastic sheet on its screen that helps it pass for colored. I can hear my mother calling me from behind the screen door, too, telling me to come inside before dark. I never hear of anyone having to be inside before dark anymore.

And with that thought, my eyes slowly open as my mom's voice metamorphoses into that of my wife's calling me in to dinner. I'm back on my front porch of today again. But I'm not sad, longing for the past. I know that no matter where one might be, it's nice to have a front porch, any front porch, and all the sights and sounds and smells that come with it. It's just nice to visit other people's porches, too.

Businesses along Messanie Street still thriving in memories

It's hard to believe that Messanie Street, between 15th and 19th Streets, once was a thriving black business section.

Kids today probably only know it for the lone tavern, the many vacant lots, and the few houses that aren't red-tagged. But as a kid growing up in the 1960's, I knew it was a place full of colorful people moving to the rhythm of the many taverns, eating places, and barber shops.

It was like Norman Rockwell with an R&B strut. Young black teenagers would hang out on the Teen Town steps in their do-rags and wrap-around shades, snapping their fingers to the tunes coming from the jukebox inside. It could be "Tighten Up" by Archie Bell and the Drells or "Super Bad" by James Brown. Whatever was playing, you knew it was the newest. Vernon "Slick" Gamble always had the latest 45s. And he also made the best hamburgers anywhere. Being able to hang out in Slick Gamble's Teen Town was a rite of passage. You knew you were a teenager if he didn't run you off.

Older folks hung out at the American Legion across the street. From here, you could hear the blues of Bobby Blue Band or B.B. King billowing out the doors. On Friday and Saturday nights, there'd be so many folks going in and out of this place, it looked like a huge black anthill from my Aunt Bobbie and Uncle Phil King's apartment window above Teen Town.

During the day, we kids would play football in the lot beside the American Legion for an unaffected audience of winos sleeping it off against the building. The smell of fried fish and chicken was usually the only thing billowing out of Big John's Chicken House. If you had the money, you could get a chicken-breast dinner from Big John's where the chicken breast was so big, it covered the plate. If you were running short on change, you could get a chicken sandwich, which was a leg or thigh doused in Trappey's hot sauce wrapped in a single slice of bread.

In Milton Bundy's tavern, they played cards. In Bunker Pennell's bar, folks danced. Both did a good business.

You might have to wait all day to get your hair cut, if you were a kid in Henry Matthew's barbershop. But no one minded. There were always cartoons on the TV and old men playing checkers in the corner. No one ever cussed in Henry's barbershop. He had signs all over the walls that forbade it.

You might get in the chair quicker at Charlie Taylor's barbershop down the street, but you might get the strap quicker too if you acted up in his shop.

A kid could get a whipping all up and down Messanie Street in those days by any adult that caught you acting up and get one for the same offense from your folks when you get home.

Networking isn't a new term to black kids who grew up along Messanie Street in those days. Adults worked together to keep all of us kids in line then.

For a time, taps on shoes were cool.

They were basically put on shoes with run-down, well-worn heels so you wouldn't have to lie down to put them on.

But hip folks would put them on new shoes because the sound they made when you strutted on concrete was cool. And, there was no other place to get them other than at Drake's Shoe Store. He knew just how to put them on and how to shine them too.

I never fail to think of all these things every time I drive down that street.

Alonzo's mom has seen it all at the drugstore from the 1st day

When Osco Drug closes its doors this weekend, it will be like losing a family member for me.

I can remember seeing my grandmother get off the bus after working all day as a short-order cook at Katz snack bar. She would always smell like cooking grease and fried food. My mom, Florence Weston, started at 85 cents an hour when Katz Drugstore opened in the East Hills Mall in 1965. And she had to work her way up to cooking.

"When I started out, they didn't have anybody that knew how to run the dishwashing machine. I said that I would run it if they gave me a raise," my mom said. "I went up to 95 cents an hour."

In each of its incarnations, as Katz Drugstore, Skaggs Drugstore to finally Osco Drugs, there has always been a Weston working there.

But only my mom has been there from the first day.

She still remembers that day.

"I can remember it well. I even know what I wore that first day. I wore a brown two-piece, a skirt, and a vest to match. The reason I can remember it so well is because there is a story behind it."

The story is that my mom, who was working on a dishwashing machine that first day, couldn't be found by any of the store bosses for a long while. She wasn't goofing off anywhere, but I guess you could say she was fitting in with the environment.

"I was working in under the dishwashing machine, and they were looking for me, but couldn't see me because my brown outfit blended in with my brown complexion in a way that they couldn't see me," she laughed.

It's been all in the family. My grandmother, Lena Weston, began working for the Kansas City-based Katz Drugstore a year after it opened its St. Joseph chain in 1946 at Sixth and Edmond Streets. It's the building that Esther's Fabric occupies now. My mother, two aunts and an uncle also worked there as teenagers.

When Katz opened another store at East Hills Shopping Center when the mall opened in 1965, my mother was one of their first hires. She was there when it changed owners and became Skaggs Drugstore in the early 1970s. She will see it close as Osco Drugs, as the only one that has worked there from the beginning.

"It was Katz Store No. 21 when it opened here in the mall. The Katz downtown was called Katz Store No. 4," said my mom.

The old store has attic space in my mind. I remember that a lot of what we owned was stuff bought on lay away from Katz Drugstore. We always got our school supplies and our flame-retardant Halloween costumes there.

I remember the Mall opened with a flourish—and Flipper, the famous TV dolphin. My mom had me ride the new East Hills bus out to see where she worked. I remember the whole place smelled like popcorn, candy, and new stuff. The smell still lingers in my mind.

East Hills was the village where I grew up in many ways. If I acted up, everyone knew my mother, and she would hear about it.

Going to the mall had always been like going to grandmother's house for my kids.

Behind the register at Osco Drug is where she saw many of the new outfits and toys at the Mall. It's also where my mom met a lot of her friends.

"I told a lot of my customers that I'm going to miss them, so I guess I'm going to have to walk in the Mall to see them," my mom said. "I'll miss all the workers at the Mall too. It won't be the same."

Summers were better when having less was having more

Summer doesn't mean as much to me now. I have more toys and more money than I did when I was a kid, but it isn't as much fun.

For one thing, we have summer-like weather off and on all year. And the wonders of technology let us swim in January and play soccer on Christmas, both indoors. Heck, we can get fruit we want anytime, thanks to the local mega-mart.

But summers when I was a kid in grade school were all about anticipation and fun that cost much less than the $10 most kids need now.

The first sounds of summer for me would come with the classroom windows making that stiff, scrunching noise as they were being raised after a long winter. The sweet and gentle breeze that came through would animate the colored construction paper birds, bees and flowers already hanging on the walls. They all had the names of the classmates who created them written in crayon on the back. That way they'd know where they'd spend their summer. Some would make it to a refrigerator door, others would be found blowing aimlessly on the streets, a reminder of that last art assignment of the school year.

We'd already decided that we'd take home the safety scissors and the apron, but throw away the paint box that was out of red and the crayons with all the paper peeled off by the time the final school bell of the year rang.

And we'd be ready for three months of Saturdays. Every day would be a new adventure, and we'd go wherever a sunny day would take us.

More often than not, it would be up on Devil's Backbone Hill. We'd ride our bikes up there when it was truly a hill, with tunnels and caves and other boys having dirt clod fights.

Sometimes we'd ride all the way back home to Kool-Aid and lunchmeat sandwiches. You could buy 50 cents worth of lunchmeat then and a pack of Kool-Aid for a nickel. That would be enough to feed you and a few of your friends. If it wasn't, we always knew what fruit was in season and who had what kind of fruit tree in their yards, and we'd go there to supplement our appetites.

We lived for the days when coupons would come in the mail. The stores would give you half-price for the face value of the coupon. If everybody got coupons on the same day, we would have a junk food fest.

Pushing lawnmowers all over town was part of summer, too. You had to if you wanted money to buy pop or candy or go swimming at Noyes pool. And Noyes pool was where you wanted to be when it got so hot that a cherry bomb pop from the ice cream man and a water hose wouldn't cut the heat.

But the heat somehow never bothered us when we played pick-up basketball games in the alley behind our house. Our court was made up of fine dust and driveway gravel. The goal was fastened to a piece of ply board that was nailed to a tree. It was more than enough for a game of "21" or "HORSE."

We would play until the lightning bugs shone in late evening. It was my grandmother's voice mixed in with the "scree, scree, scree" sound of the cicadas that called us home before dark.

We'd sometimes have lunchmeat sandwiches again for supper, because it would still be too hot to cook. And when we finished eating, we watched whatever was on television at the time. Being able to tape our favorite shows and watch them anytime is fine, but I think it somehow makes them less special. The anticipation is gone.

We hear some kids today who have more toys and more summer activities than we ever knew existed say they're bored. And I believe it. Sometimes having less is having more.

Present day Halloween just doesn't compare to the old days

There was a time when Halloween was not looked upon as a sinister and evil holiday. When there were no sanitized, lighted shopping malls for kids to trick-or-treat in. When kids could walk the streets late at night and worry, not about getting abducted, but about getting enough candy to last in school for a few weeks.

I remember we trusted our neighbors not to put razor blades in our apples or poison our candy—even if we did tease their dog.

My grandmother used to work at the old Katz drug store, and she'd get all the grandchildren's costumes on discount. But she could have them all on layaway since July, for all we knew.

We didn't care. All we thought about was tearing open that square cardboard box with cellophane over the front and getting to the neat mask and costume inside.

There was a time we, or should I say I, actually thought that people would mistake me for whatever creature or hero's costume I had on. I knew Frankenstein didn't wear a lime green flame-retardant suit that laced up the back and had his name written in sparkle glitter on the front. I knew that his face wasn't made out of hard plastic and fastened to his head with a rubber band. But I figured the grown-ups were dumb enough to fall for it. After all, they oohed and ahhed, "look at Frankenstein" or "look at that uh, uh, minstrel hobo, is it?"

Some years, money was short, and there was none for a store-bought costume. So some of us put on our old outgrown clothes, cut them up, put fake blood on them, and black grease paint on our faces. (No, the Carnahan boys weren't with us.)

We never quite figured out what that get-up was supposed to look like, but it got us just as much candy as if we had a store-bought costume on.

And all we wanted was candy. Good candy. Not those taffy things wrapped in black and orange wax paper that somehow showed up in every bag and never got eaten. Not those orange marshmallowy things that are supposed to look and taste like peanuts, but don't. We wanted candy bars, Lik-A-Maids, Jujubes, and Chick-O-Sticks.

If we got apples and oranges, we gave them to our parents or traded them with some dumb kid for his candy. Popcorn balls? They were good for throwing at other kids.

The weirdest thing I was ever offered on Halloween was a can of beer. I got it from this weird old guy in the neighborhood whose dog we used to tease. He didn't have his porch light on, but we went up and knocked on his door anyway on a dare. I gave the beer to a wild and crazy uncle who I thought would really appreciate something like that.

I was going to stop trick-or-treating way before I got to high school until I saw a guy who was a sophomore junior-varsity basketball player carrying a bag full of candy.

I trick-or-treated clear up until I was a junior in high school. I was slick about it though. I would take my little cousins trick-or-treating and the people would give me candy too. I'm too old to trick-or-treat now, and my kids are too old, too. I look at all the costumes now and it's Freddie Kruger, the Scream guy, the Silence of the Lambs guy or some politician.

And I see them as signs of our times. We live in times where real life horrors are often scarier than what any horror writer can dream up. Pick up the newspaper, turn on the news—it very well could be Halloween every day. But we make sure we're extra safe on October 31st.

Memories fill the gaps in neighborhood decimated by time

The writer Thomas Wolfe said you can't go home again, but I did it anyway Sunday afternoon.

To be more precise, I went back home to my old neighborhood. I went there to visit a childhood friend who was sitting with and taking care of his terminally ill mother.

There were four generations in that house Sunday. My friend's mother, my friend, my friend's niece and her daughter. That was a living testament to how long his family had been here. To honor their privacy, I won't mention any names.

My friend's mother is one of the few people that stayed in the old neighborhood. Many families, including my own who grew up here, have long since packed up and left to make neighborhoods somewhere else.

Where once sat houses with people inside and cars and trucks out front are now empty lots. Houses become empty lots so fast here, you have to wonder if some folks didn't just pack up their homes and take them too when they left. Many of those left behind have boards for windows now.

Years ago, the small white house my friend grew up in and where his mother still lives was as quiet and unassuming as the other homes on the block. It stands out now like one of a few good molars still left in a mouth full of missing and decayed teeth.

Somehow the living room here seemed much smaller Sunday than I remembered it. We could talk in whispers and still be heard over the Knicks game on TV. A couple of leaps could put you in the kitchen.

My friend and I both remembered the days when pushing a toy car across the floor felt like taking a cross-country trip across a carpet desert. It seemed that huge.

Even when we became teenagers it still seemed large.

It was large enough to become a dance floor for 20 or more of our friends on a Saturday night.

It is large enough now for my friend's 2-year-old great niece.

There were still places underneath the coffee table she hadn't been yet.

Even the alley behind the house seemed much smaller and tamer now. When we were kids playing there, it was truly an urban jungle with lots of trees and brush. It was also a shortcut from my house to my aunt's house on Messanie Street.

My friend could remember disappearing into the jungle once in an attempt to beat his father undetected. He was never allowed on Messanie Street and the alley always provided good cover between the then busy street and his bedroom.

After all these years there's still an old plywood backboard nailed to a tree. It's in the backyard of a neighbor who is no longer there.

We would close our eyes and imagine the sounds of kids playing in that alley and of mothers calling those children in for lunch or supper. With our eyes closed we can see their faces.

My friend said his mother sometimes talks of seeing people who have long since gone. He's not sure if she's seeing ghosts or just having vivid memories.

Sometimes it's too hard for any of us to tell the difference.

This past month, in my weekly "Tales of the Midland Empire" feature, I tried to focus on local black history items in honor of Black History Month.

While doing my research for these stories, I found a desire in many people to know more about local black history. A few people shared photos and memories with me.

I said this many times before, and I'll say it again. I think it's time for a book about local black history that tells all about the black schools, Messanie Street, the black South Side and the black North Side and famous and infamous St. Joseph blacks.

I would like to take on this mission, but I need lots of help.

'God bless Ms. Judy in heaven' says writing on the box where she shared

Love is the currency of heaven. But Judy Benning spent it lavishly on earth. And she gave it away generously to people in need.

No sign anywhere said the crumbling, tiny brick building with a leaky roof and space heater at 214 W. Missouri Avenue was called Judy's Care and Share Shop.

Folks around just knew that Ms. Benning cared. And they knew she shared whatever she had—clothing, furniture, money, and God's love. She gave out of that shop and out of her heart.

"Listen, this woman, if you walked up to her, told her you had no shoes to wear, she'd take hers off and give them to you," said Bonnie Chavez, who had known Ms. Benning for more than 20 years. "She lived a meager life because she gave everything away to other people."

Mrs. Chavez works in the Sack and Save deli nearby.

She saw Ms. Benning Saturday. She didn't know that would be the last time.

Early Monday morning, Ms. Benning was struck and killed by a hit-and-run vehicle as she walked down an Elwood, Kansas road. The 74-year-old former schoolteacher and nurse's aide was pronounced dead at the scene.

By Tuesday afternoon, several plastic flowers, thrift store wreaths, and handwritten notes of appreciation covered the dilapidated front door of the tiny Care and Share building.

A photo of a black Labrador ripped from a magazine was taped to one wall with a message handwritten in black marker that just read: "My Friend Forever. Uncle Bud 1989-1999."

One cardboard sign, which looked like it had been tacked to the building ever since Ms. Benning opened the place more than 12 years ago, simply said: "Please Do Not Drop Off Any Items When We Are Closed. Thank You."

As always, old furniture and clothing cluttered the small dirt yard next to the building, waiting to be wanted.

A cardboard box filled with clothes too small or too old sat on an abandoned couch covered in print fabric not many could want.

On the cardboard box someone wrote: "God Bless Ms. Judy in Heaven."

All abandoned and unwanted and in need. Who would take them now? Who would care?

Jerri Artis and Madilyn Atchison wondered that too, as they got out of their vehicles and stood in front of the solemn building.

Both women remembered a lady who helped them when they needed it most.

They reminisced between tears.

"Most everything in my house is furnished from the stuff she gave me, and she gave me and my kids clothes too," Ms. Artis said. "I don't think any person had a better heart in St. Joseph."

Madilyn spoke of how she met Ms. Benning three years ago when she came to the shop needing clothes. In gratitude, she would haul junk away for her.

"I hauled off a load for her last week," she sobbed. "She was just like a mother to me."

So quiet the place seemed now. No kids rushing out the fragile wooden door with new used toys in hand. No stray cats hanging around because no one else could remember to put out a dish of milk.

The old white Dodge van with the plastic animals glued on it wasn't there either. It won't be again.

The Bible speaks of a rich man asking Jesus how to get into heaven. Jesus tells the man to sell his possessions, give to the poor, and follow him. He would receive his treasure in heaven.

The rich man found that too hard. He went away sad. Mrs. Chavez and everyone else who knew Ms. Benning knows that she went away happy.

"I told her once she's got a sure place in heaven," Mrs. Chavez said. "And she said, 'You don't have to have material items to be happy on earth.' If people would be more giving and not worry about material items, I think there would be a lot more happiness."

Blues comes from pain

To play the blues well, some say you have to know pain on a first-name basis. It's even better if you call it kin.

Knowing pain that way gets the blues in your blood. In spite of the pain, or working alongside it, the blues drive whoever possesses them to tell their story.

Misery loves company. The blues love an audience.

Blues guitarist B.B. King once said, "The blues is pain, but it's a pain that brings joy."

Rock bassist and vocalist Bugsy Maugh and guitarist Jerry Forney brought joy to a crowded room at Magoon's on Saturday evening.

Forney showed up with a few other local musicians to play for Bugsy's CD release party.

Forney's house caught fire the night before. Since then, home for him has been the couch of friends. Forney entertained the crowd with that pain Saturday night. It fueled his licks. It bent the notes for him. Still, what makes a man come out and play the blues less than a day after his house caught fire?

"Well, because it was Bugsy and I didn't want to sit around and think about it anymore. I figured it'd do me good to get out and go, so I did," Forney said.

Some of Bugsy's pain comes from being diagnosed with lung cancer about 15 years ago. The disease left him with two half-lungs and eight ribs.

Cancer didn't even try to take his spirit. It knew there would be a hell of a fight if it tried to rip the blues out.

After the cancer came, every performance was always Bugsy's last. I heard it so much I lost count. Bugsy's wife, Carolyn, said each performance wore him out. It usually takes him two or three days to recover.

I won't hear from Bugsy for months. Then out of the blue, that raspy, wheezing-for-air voice will be on the other line: "I'm playing again." "It's my last time." "For real this time." "I can't do it anymore." I heard that about a year ago.

There Bugsy was Saturday night, with oxygen tubes coming out of his nose, wailing the blues away. His fingers ever nimble on rhythm guitar. His mind still sharp enough to school a bass player on the chord changes.

Sometimes the oxygen tubes slipped out of Bugsy's nose while he sang. A band mate positioned them back in.

Asking Bugsy why is like asking him why he likes to eat, walk or breathe. The blues are just as essential to his being.

He'll just laugh or mumble an answer.

Forney, too, took his pain in stride. What causes the blues is part of life. Go with it, roll with it. Make music about it.

A fire can take away a lot of things. And it did.

"I got my guitars out of there. I got the stuff that mattered to me," he said.

That house was built in 1872. It's a historic home in Hopkins, Mo.

"That house where I live is Matthew and Phoebe Roseberry's house. That street was named after them. They, like, settled that town up there in 1872," Forney said.

Forney said he'll get help from the town folks to help restore his home. He's pretty handy, too. But he didn't have insurance. He needs more help.

There was a fundraiser for Jerry Forney at Magoon's Famous Delicatessen. The plan was for local and area musicians to have a blues jam in support of their brother and provide entertainment for the crowd while they're at it.

It will be from a pain that provides joy.

Man who thought he was Jesus found himself again

Samir (not his real name) thought he was Jesus. If you believed him, you had to believe that Jesus was black, stood about 6 feet 5 inches tall and wore jeans.

When the Sudanese native was arrested in September 2010 on a disorderly conduct charge, that's how he identified himself. For more than two months, doctors at the Heartland Regional Medical Center Mental Health Unit treated him not as a deity, but as a paranoid schizophrenic.

Strong drugs and heavy counseling could not change Samir's mind. He was Jesus, you fools. And he carried a Bible to prove it.

I heard about Samir after Public Administrator Bill McMurray became his emergency guardian that October. He also was placed in the mental health unit in October.

But Samir's problem was so severe he needed long-term treatment. Heartland's mental health unit at the time only had 24 beds and the average length of stay was a week. All the long-term facilities in the area were full.

"This is Christmas, and there is no room at the inn," Dr. Charles Shuman, Heartland Medical Director, said in a December 13, 2010 article.

Heartland officials set up a meeting for me with Samir. At the time, I found him to be well spoken and composed. I wasn't sure how much of the composure was medicinally engineered, but he seemed pleasant enough.

When I asked his name, he said, "Jesus," and said it with the same confidence I have in knowing that my name is Alonzo. His piercing look dared anyone who doubted it.

Now, I've gone to church enough to hear and believe that God can come in the form of any person, so that's why you'd better be nice to everybody. As a result, my doubt wavered for a brief instant.

But there was nothing to make me believe Samir actually was Jesus. There was no miracle to be seen or parable to be learned from being arrested for standing in the middle of Frederick Avenue and getting arrested for disorderly conduct. I couldn't believe that's what Jesus would do.

Yet, Samir was a child of God—just like all of us.

I lost track of whatever happened to Samir. The people treating him didn't want to share anything with the media for fear it might hinder his progress.

A few weeks ago, I ran into Mr. McMurray and he told me what had happened to Samir. He said the Family Guidance ACT (Assertive Community Treatment) team did a tremendous job bringing Samir back to who he was. His guardianship was terminated, he got a job, bought a car and was able to leave residential care and move in with a cousin.

"He improved tremendously," Mr. McMurray said.

He quit his job in March 2012 and moved back to the Sudan with his cousin in April to be with his father.

But the Sudan can be a dangerous place, Mr. McMurray said. It still is a place of much civil unrest.

"I wonder, 'my gosh, I hope he's alive.' He's OK, but it is a great success story," he said.

"This is exactly what the Mental Health Unit at Heartland, Family Guidance and Community Mental Health Services is supposed to do," Mr. McMurray added. "If somebody is ill, help them manage their illness and become a productive member of society."

Samir was a man who was so deeply mentally ill that not many thought he would make it back. But some people did. From their love and hard work, a man who once was lost was found again.

Mardi Gras is not for children, seriously

A lady called in last week asking people to pray against the Mardi Gras parade, Mark Sheehan and myself. Now isn't that enough to make you feel like a national disaster? I know it did me.

I've been prayed for many times. And I've been told plenty times to go where prayers can't reach me. But I don't think I've ever had anyone pray against me before. So that sort of puts not only me, but also Mark Sheehan and the whole Coleman Hawkins Jazz Heritage Society in the same social group with hurricanes, floods and locust plagues.

And it's all because of the Mardi Gras parade.

This pious woman isn't alone. There're quite a few people upset from rumors they've heard about our Coleman Hawkins Mardi Gras parade.

They're hearing rumors that our parade is one big bacchanalian orgy, one that would do the Roman Emperor Caligula proud. The rumors sound like the back cover of a pulp fiction novel. Public nudity! Rampant sex! Teenage girls doing the unthinkable!

Many of these rumors can be traced back to one woman who brought her grade-school-age niece down to watch the whole parade one year. And this is after we repeatedly said that the parade wasn't for children. Never mind that it was in a bar district late on a Saturday at night.

Now, I'm not going to lie to you and say the Mardi Gras parade is just a bunch of folks holding hands and singing gospel hymns and church spirituals. It's not.

There are women who expose their breasts. There is drinking. These are adults.

Some are responsible. Some are not.

But we're all not hedonistic heathens, either. Most, if not all of us, do go to church. We believe in God too.

But I've never seen any teenage girls perform any lewd acts in the parade. In fact, if that were to happen, I'm sure there are enough responsible citizens at the parade to make sure that they stop.

Besides, how does anybody know if there are teenage girls at the parade baring their breasts if they don't know their names? If you don't know their names, then how can you know their ages? If you do know the girls' names, then why not report their parents for being irresponsible? That is why we repeatedly stress that the parade is for adults, because adult things might happen. There are plenty of places where adult things happen and kids aren't allowed or shouldn't be allowed, like bars. And Mardi Gras happens in a bar district after curfew.

Now the City Council wants us to meet with the people who are against the parade. What for? As soon as our side walks in the door, it's going to look as though we've come to defend immorality.

Really, all we ever wanted to do in the first place was raise money for our June jazz festival and give people an opportunity to act silly and have a good time.

If you're offended by breasts, then don't go to an art gallery and don't come to the Mardi Gras parade because you might see a couple.

We don't condone it. It happens. But that's about the worst that happens. Besides, who hasn't seen a woman breast feed in public?

No one is married to Mardi Gras. Not one of our Coleman Hawkins Jazz Society members exchanged any vows to remain faithful to it.

Shut it down if you need to and congratulate yourself on keeping St. Joseph safe from rumors of gross immorality, safe from revelry and safe from God's condemnation.

Some people will no doubt grandly proclaim it a moral victory if they get the Mardi Gras parade shut down. They'll feel that they truly did the Lord's work.

That's OK with me. If they spared God that dirty menial task, then maybe they did. I'm sure he has bigger tasks at hand. And so do we. There are more important things to worry about in our community than a parade, things like babies being killed, people going hungry and finding shelter for the homeless.

For me that puts the whole thing in perspective.

Shutting down a parade isn't a big deal. I've seen stray dogs and disoriented drivers do that.

JUST FOR LAUGHS

What, get negative about autumn? That's definitely no problem

I could wax poetic about the virtues of fall. I could write some heartfelt prose about the beautiful trees ablaze in splendor, the crisp, fresh air and the bright, blue autumn sky. I could write about football, smiling pumpkins, hardy mums and the smell of burning leaves.

But I won't. Anybody can write about that stuff. I have. My wife tells me I can find negative in anything. So I will. I'll find negative in autumn even though it's my favorite season. If I'm destined to grow into a curmudgeonly, old man, then I need practice.

Pray for me.

If you live next to a school like I do, then you know how hard it is to find a place to park on weekday fall afternoons. Cars and vans filled with mothers picking up their children from school are all over the neighborhood and in my driveway.

When I finally get to come home after circling the block several times for a parking space, my front yard looks like hurricane Dennis just passed through—but a juvenile hurricane Dennis. It doesn't leave the usual broken tree limbs, trailers and junk cars and cows, like grown-up hurricanes and tornadoes. Instead, this hurricane leaves candy wrappers, construction paper art projects and bad test papers in its wake and in my yard.

Sure, that crisp, nippy autumn air feels nice and invigorating—until it starts whistling through the cracks in your house. Autumn means winterizing time, and that means work. You have to pull the air conditioners out of the windows and haul them down to the basement storage area. You have to caulk all your windows and doors. The $30.00 you'd saved back for some CDs or a video game has to go to the furnace man now because you can never get the damn thing started. As each of those crisp, lovely autumn days go by, each gas bill gets higher and higher.

You've had three seasons to get over the Kansas City Chiefs' last bumbling, stumbling season. Fall is back again, and you're reminded again just how incompetent they can be or will be. You now have to prepare for three months of hoarseness from screaming at Elvis Grbac, Gunther Cunningham or any number of other Chiefs for making boneheaded moves. You'd also better be ready to listen to every yahoo in a Chiefs jacket tell you how stupid the team is and what they would do better.

The lovely, colorful leaves look pretty on the trees.

They'd look even better if they just stayed on the trees.

Somebody has to rake up all those dead leaves, and you know it will be you. You know exactly what you will be doing on the first open burning weekend. You'll be raking up leaves and tearing out dead tomato plants and trying to find a city open-burning ordinance-approved container to burn them in. By the time you find a container suitable enough to keep you from getting arrested by a cop who has nothing better to do than watch people burn leaves, you realize how much time you could have saved by just grinding up the leaves with your lawnmower. And you still have to pull up the bulbs and seed the lawn while you're missing I don't know how many great college football games on TV.

See? It doesn't take much negativity to trash a beautiful season. And winter will be even easier to hate.

Those old comic-book ads may have given birth to our cynicism

Many of us Americans have become cynical and doubting like never before. And, we may have good reasons.

You can't trust our leaders when you can pick up the newspaper or turn on the TV at any given time and expect to see any number of them caught in a scandal. The Surgeon General, or whoever it is that tells us certain things are bad for us, changes his or her mind daily. The weatherman tells us it's going to be sunny, and we walk out into a thunderstorm. We haven't been able to tell if it's butter or if it's margarine for a long time now. It's been said, at one time or another, that all of these things add to our national distrust.

I have another reason. It's one that has been overlooked by many experts and may well be the driving force behind our recent poverty of trust. Are you ready for this? Drum roll, please. I believe the major culprit in our faith theft is… those ads they put in the back of comic books.

That's right. Those back-of-the-comic-book ads that many of us in the baby boomer generation grew up believing in. We got burned on those ads, and we pass this wisdom on to the next generation. We tell our kids that the toy they see and want on TV won't work like the commercial says it will. We want to spare them the same heartache we once experienced after we finally got the sea monkeys we ordered months ago out of the back of a "Turok, Son of Stone" comic book in the mail.

In the comic book ad they look like cute web-footed monkeys about the size of a large gold fish. The ad said you'd be entertained for hours by watching these neat little creatures do flips, somersaults, and other acrobatics in your fish bowl.

But, you know better—now. The neat little creatures were just little dots, zigzagging in the water. And you never figured out what those dots actually were. They could have been water gnats or some other bug that, if your mom found out about it, would make you take them out of the house.

I sent off for a pair of X-ray glasses once. The ad showed a picture of a guy looking through a woman's dress. I thought at the time that it would be great to take to school. I'd be able to see what the teacher and all the girls in my class really looked like.

Those were a joke, too. Instead of being a pre-pubescent boy's dream, they were a rip-off. The glasses didn't allow you to see through people's clothes at all. They put a fuzzy outline around everything, as if you were looking at a skeleton of something. You'd be fooled if you looked at your hand. When you looked at anything else, it looked like an aura around it.

I never sent off for the Joe Weider stuff they advertised.

You remember the ad. It showed the picture of a skinny guy getting sand kicked in his face by some muscle-bound hulk as he took his girlfriend. The ad said that if you'd buy the Joe Weider plan or whatever, you'd become a big brute too and be able to kick sand and take someone else's girlfriend.

I never bought in to that, but I have a friend who unfortunately did. Not too long ago, he told me, with tears running down his cheeks, that that too was a sham. All it was was a pamphlet telling you common sense stuff to do like take a bath, eat right and be regular. Really.

I'll bet you that some guy around my age complained.

I'm sorry I didn't see the customized sign in front of your parking space

I knew it would happen sooner or later—designated parking for people other than the handicapped and the clergy.

If you've shopped at Wal-Mart recently, you may have noticed designated spots available for parents with sick children.

The signs have no symbol like the ones for handicapped parking, just the words, "Parking for parents with sick children."

I was intrigued by these new signs, so I called the main offices for Wal-Mart in Bentonville, Arkansas to ask if there were any other types of signs in any other Wal-Mart stores and to ask why they decided to make designated areas in their parking lots.

I discovered there are other designated areas in other Wal-Marts across the country.

"In some Super Centers, we have pharmacy parking spaces designated for pharmacy customers, and in some inner-city stores, we have police substations in the store and parking space designated for those officers," Wal-Mart spokesman Brian Holdberg said. "It's something we're trying to do as another service to our customers. Our goal at Wal-Mart is to make the shopping experience as pleasant as it can be."

This is a very good idea.

It's very commendable and admirable for a shopping center to be so compassionate toward its users. If I had a sick child or my wife were pregnant or I needed a prescription filled or if I were a policeman, I'd more than welcome the convenience. But by the same token, I can see this whole thing getting out of hand, if not at Wal-Mart, then at some other shopping centers that copies the effort. Here are some possibilities:

PARKING FOR PARENTS WITH BAD KIDS AT DAY-CARE CENTERS: These signs would have icons similar to the popular decal on truck windows of a bad little boy urin... er... relieving himself on everything from Chevys to Kansas City Chiefs. The parking spaces here would be set up facing away from the front of the day-care center to being in time-out for the rest of the day.

PARKING FOR DRUNK DRIVERS AT BARS, RESTAURANTS AND SPORTING ARENAS: These signs would have a stick man throwing a beer bottle out the window of a truck. They would be situated at an open field behind these places.

PARKING FOR PEOPLE WHO ARE JUST PLAIN LAZY AND INCONSIDERATE: A stick man sitting in a chair holding a remote would designate where these people may park.

PARKING FOR OFFICE BROWN-NOSERS: This would simply have a pair of lips. The designated space would be directly behind the chief executive's office or plant manager's parking space.

PARKING FOR ALL-DAY SHOPPERS: The people's names would be put on signs in areas behind the store.

These are just a few I can imagine. I'm sure some of these stores will have a better imagination than I do before long.

I am prejudiced

Excuse me, but I am prejudiced. I say that with the conviction of a drunk facing the sober truth at an Alcoholic's Anonymous meeting.

It usually takes a drink or a binge that ends in disaster to convince a drinker that he's an alcoholic. For me, it took one more plane trip to confirm my narrow-mindedness. Or I should say, my darling wife to confirm it for me.

But before I say anything about my revelatory plane trip to Washington, D.C. last week, let me make it perfectly clear that I am not a racist. Yeah, I know that sounds a little like Richard Nixon saying I am not a crook right before he got busted at Watergate. But it's true. A racist or bigot hates someone because of his or her race or color. I don't hate anybody.

But I'm truly sorry to admit that sometimes I have a problem with prejudging people. And Lord knows that I know being prejudiced isn't right. I can't count the times someone has looked at me as if I'm every black man they've ever seen robbing and murdering on the evening news. I've had people snatch up their kids and lock their car doors when I walk by.

I like to think some of that goodness my mother worked hard to instill in me with a belt and a Bible shows somewhere. After all, I did pay for it. But there I was at the Kansas City airport last week acting like a dark-complexioned Archie Bunker.

I fought hard not to think that every swarthy-skinned person I saw looked like the September 11 hijackers. But Mexicans, light-skinned black dudes and white guys with good tans even became suspects.

And just our luck, my wife and I found our seats on the Express jet directly behind two brown-skinned guys with

90

black hair. One of them had a harmless looking laptop computer. The other had a small Palm Pilot.

But to a mind dizzy from too much Republican spin, they became weapons of mass destruction. Were they punching in codes to set off a bomb? Did I really see them look at each other and wink?

I remembered on one flight to Nashville last summer, I saw two guys who looked just like these two get up and go to the back of the plane at the same time. I just knew they were going back to set off a bomb. I was so sure that I even warned the guy sitting in the window seat beside me about it. He just shook his head and turned away from me, the unpatriotic simp.

Luckily those guys didn't do anything that time. But now they might try something I thought. I warned my wife. But she, too, shook her head and turned away from me after I reached in my briefcase and pulled out an ink pen. "This is our defense in case they try anything," I whispered to her. She stifled a laugh.

After it was OK to turn on computers and other electronic devices the laptop guy quickly went to work. I peered through the seats and made out something about home loans on the tiny computer screen. I figured that was just a phony screen saver to throw me off to what he was really up to. No good!

I looked over and caught the Palm Pilot guy feverishly pressing buttons on his hand-held device. Crap! He's punching in coordinates!

Now I had to work out a plan. There was a big American-looking guy snoozing a few seats away. I figured I could wake him up and we could tag-team both those swarthy guys out and land the plane safely. Luckily, I didn't need his help. We landed safely at Reagan International Airport anyway. Turns out the two swarthy guys really were white guys with tans. They had wives and kids running to greet them when they got off the plane. My wife ran to the baggage claim, laughing her head off.

Yeah, I do feel like a big fool now, a very ashamed one too. But I still catch myself thinking sometimes that those guys knew better than to try anything around me.

Smile more

When I walked into the convenience store the other day, all I wanted was a cup of coffee and a USA Today newspaper. The clerk threw in some free advice.

"You need to smile more," she said.

So I paid her with a smile and some loose pocket change before turning to walk out the door.

Like the catchy melody of a song you can't get out of your head, the woman's remark stuck with me all day. I became self-conscious about how often I smiled. I noticed how many times other people smiled at me.

By the end of the day, smiling just seemed a bit too overrated.

I only have so many smiles for rude people and rude drivers. After a while, they just have to take what's left and sometimes that isn't good.

Now don't get me wrong. I think smiling is virtuous. Doctors even tell you it's better for your health to smile. Ministers tell you it's good for your soul. But I don't think it's good to smile all the time. And that's what I feel much of society thinks we all need to do.

Have a Coke and a smile. Don't worry, be happy. Take Prozac.

I think if you smile too much, people will think you're nuts, you're up to something or you're on something. You can smile or laugh at the wrong time or the wrong person, too.

Smile or laugh at Mike Tyson and see what happens. You won't have a nice day.

You'll need a good doctor and a tetanus shot.

Do you think anyone ever tells Clint Eastwood to smile? If they do, I'm sure they'll end up making his day.

I think smiles lose their impact if they're used all the time. How often do you smile back at the waitress in the fast-food place who asks can she help you? How sincere do you think some of their smiles are at the end of an eight-hour shift?

Still, I know people who smile a lot and are truly sincere. It's part of their nature. St. Joseph School District Superintendent Dan Colgan comes to mind. So does Jean "Miz Jean" Robinson, the grandmother of Carolina Panther and former Benton High School football player Mike Rucker.

They both have smiles that can light up any room.

But some of the greatest smiles come from people who don't normally smile.

Take the actor Harry Dean Stanton.

He is known for his hangdog expression. But when he does smile, it feels like a glass of warm milk on a cold night. It just seems comforting and genuine.

My mother likes to tell people that something really had to be funny to make me laugh as a kid. I would clown around and cut up, but I wouldn't laugh or smile at just anything.

It usually took Red Skelton, the Three Stooges or my Uncle Tommy McGaughy to do the trick.

But what I suspect my mother probably means is that I was a kid who never got the joke. And if I did, it would be years later and at the wrong time, like when a police officer is writing me out a speeding ticket.

Lots of times the reason I don't smile now is because I'm in deep thought. It's not the Socrates or Einstein kind of deep thinking. It's more like the "Where did I leave my car keys?" or "Did I turn off the stove?" type of introspection.

Next time any of you readers see me somewhere and I'm not smiling, don't think I'm being rude. I've probably just lost something.

Jiffy the dog

When you visit most people's homes, one of the first things they ask is if you want a drink. You visit Mark Sheehan's home, he asks if you want a dog.

For several years, my wife, Deanna, and I have been going to Mark and Candise Sheehan's lovely home to watch Chiefs games. And every single time he has asked if we wanted to take his dog, Jiffy, home with us when we leave. I've never seen a man so bent on getting rid of his dog.

I've even got as far as my car, reached into my coat pocket for my car keys and pulled out a short, fat, black dog instead.

"We don't need another one," my wife said. I'm still not sure if she meant we didn't need another dog or was referring to me. After all, I am short, fat and black and at times I've been known to be a dog.

But anyway, we finally gave in a couple of weeks ago and agreed to keep Jiffy for a weekend.

"Try him out. See if you like him," Mark said.

Now the last time I heard that pitch it was from a used car salesman. And he, too, had that long, curling mustache, sort of like Snidely Whiplash, the bad cartoon guy.

Whenever a car salesman pushes too hard to get you to buy a certain car, you can bet your Chiefs tickets there is something wrong with the car. And you won't find out what that is until the warranty runs out.

In the case of Jiffy, I didn't find out what he was like until after Mark and Candise were already on a fast train to Jefferson City without a cell phone.

From all the many times at Mark's watching the games, I would have to describe Jiffy as a remarkably well-behaved dog. He was sort of like a Chia Pet that could walk. He seemed extremely low-maintenance.

All I ever saw the Sheehan's do was water and feed him and walk him occasionally. The rest of the time, he just sat in the corner somewhere and grew hair.

The first thing Jiffy did when he came to our house was jump into my recliner.

When I kicked him out, he ran over to the couch and began rubbing against it furiously. Before I could figure out what he was doing he ran back over to the recliner and shocked the heck out of me!

That jolted my memory. I quickly remembered Mark telling me once that Jiffy didn't chase balls or fetch anything but that he did like to shock people. Now I was beginning to figure out what I had gotten into. Jiffy was the Eddie Haskell of dogs.

He was just like the smart-aleck kid on the old "Leave It To Beaver" show who acted extremely polite and obedient when it was to his convenience. The rest of the time he was a joker.

As long as we were in the house, Jiffy usually did nothing but sleep and beg at the table. We'd leave for awhile and come back to find the phone off the hook and my wife's underclothes all over the floor. At this point, I think I should say that Jiffy is not a boy dog but a neutered girl dog. That should put your mind at ease about anything you might be thinking about the underwear part. That simple fact sure put to rest some questions I had about the dog then.

It's always easy to assume that all dogs are male because many of us, men and women, have been taught that all males are dogs. But that's another story.

I was just getting used to Jiffy when Mark and Candise came to pick her up. I wasn't there when they came but my wife said the dog was real glad to see them.

And Mark seems real glad to have Jiffy back now too. Not once has he offered me a dog since he came back. Well maybe once, along with his Chiefs tickets.

Alonzo's Catalog of St Joseph Holiday Toys
December 12, 2001

I don't know what other St. Joseph residents think, but I myself don't see much of an incentive to buy locally. Sure, I'd like to contribute to the tax base of our town and help it grow just like anyone else. But I'm on a budget and gas is cheap now. I'll leave town to look for that better deal.

And if the St. Joseph Chamber of Commerce tries to put Moe, its silly looking, blue-and-white cow mascot in my way, I'll run him over getting to the interstate. But sometimes shopping locally isn't just about saving money. Sometimes it has to do with marketing. And Jesse James and the Pony Express are tired old St. Joseph marketing tools.

We need to capitalize on other facets of our city, and we need to try and reach our youth. It would be nice to have our own line of St. Joe toys and games. Here are just a few suggestions from the Alonzo Weston Catalog of Fictitious St. Joseph Toys:

GI ST. JOE: Kids, get your Rolling Hills and St. Joseph Public Library board action figures. Dorothy Elliott, Dave Bahner, Ken Beck, George Pappas and other library board warriors come dressed in full authentic combat gear. They're all here. Collect them all.

DOWNTOWN ST. JOE BARBIE: C'mon, how realistic is it for Barbie to own a sports car, fancy clothes and a condo without a job? Downtown St. Joe Barbie doesn't work either, but she's great for teaching real life skills. The doll comes with a shopping cart full of aluminum cans, an Open Door Food Kitchen meal ticket, a rehab center graduation certificate and a St. Jo Frontier Casino boarding pass.

HEARTLAND REGIONAL MEDICAL CENTER OPERATION GAME: Kids, you too can be a Heartland hospital worker. Keep the buzzer from going off by keeping your patients in stitches with laughter. Note: Some editions of the game were shipped without a funny bone and recalled by the manufacturer.

THE MESSANIE STREET EDITION BIG WHEEL TRIKE: The Po Po ain't racial profiling when they make you hit the curb in this baby. They just want to get a better look at those smooth spoke rims and slammin' Dayton tires. Comes complete with Ghetto Blast trike stereo and static straps. Batteries not included.

WHERE'S BAKER?: Whatever happened to Charles Baker, that Midtown activist that showed so much polemic promise? Follow the map of St. Joe streets in this colorful board game to find out "Where's Baker?"

THE MAYOR LARRY STOBBS DOLL: Some dolls talk. Some dolls walk. This one talks with feet inserted in mouth. Pull the string and hear Stobbsy say a million and one (Really! Count 'em!) cute things about St. Joe pride. Comes with kung fu action grip beard.

ST. JOE POST OFFICE GAME: Who will get caught with the anthrax letter card in his hand when the bell rings? The player who has the most Kevin Kirby Red Cross cards wins. Game comes with dice, latex gloves and ambulance siren.

LET'S PLAY TRAILS WEST!: Let's see if you too can put on a huge, boring festival before drawing the Evil Ken Shearin card and losing the game.

ST. JO FRONTIER CASINO: Play all of your favorite games at your favorite casino. Lose play money instead. Comes with senior citizen discount card.

December 4, 2002

Now that we're through with Thanksgiving, it's time for giving. It's also that time of year again to thumb through the Alonzo Weston Catalog of Fictitious St. Joseph Toys.

These are toys you can find only in St. Joseph. They are made in St. Joseph by St. Joseph people who want to give that special St. Joseph gift to that special St. Joseph someone. Got that?

So why get in a fistfight at the mall trying to buy some high-priced commercial crud that every kid in the free world will find under the tree on Christmas morning? In this catalog you can find all the really neat, one-of-a-kind toys. But before you go shopping, please read this disclaimer. Everything comes with a disclaimer these days, so here's mine: Like I said before, these are entirely fictitious toys. Anyone without a sense of humor is not allowed to play with them.

Last year I tried to play Santa Claus and give some of my toys away. Instead of being grateful, the "It's your call" posse told me to get out of town. It seems like part of that group enjoys telling everyone that says something they don't like to get out of town.

Well, my hometown friends, get off the phone and look out your window. People and places are leaving town faster than you can say Quaker Oats.

Anyway, thanks for bringing me my hat and coat, but I plan on staying awhile. If I really took you folks seriously and did leave, who else would bring you such wonderful gifts?

Just look through my catalog and try to ease up and have a little fun this holiday season. Don't drink and drive. Don't fight over toys or parking spaces. Don't knock over the Christmas tree. Happy shopping.

MONOPOLY (The Mrs. Dorothy Brown version): Sure, there's no Park Place here, but you can buy the whole block of 15th and Charles! Buy one or more of these 18 Midtown lots owned by this wise and frugal lady and build up the property. Pass go and collect Community Development Block Grant Money. Game comes with "get out of jail" and "go work for Trinity Management Group" cards.

COLEMAN HAWKINS AT FELIX STREET SQUARE SCRABBLE GAME: That's not a word, or is it? See how many words you can come up with to add to the name of this popular downtown park.

TRAILS WEST! WESTWARD HO! BATTLE SET: Re-enact this new Civil War battle between the Trails West! and Westward Ho! festivals. Comes with more than 100 molded plastic action figurines of Ken Shearin, Karen Graves, John Josendale and others. Beer tents and Bud girls are optional.

THE RIVER BLUFFS REGIONAL LIBRARY PUZZLE: Puzzle comes with large, easy-to-fit pieces. However, grown-ups should not leave kids unattended who are attempting to piece together this puzzle.

DOWNTOWN ST. JOSEPH CLUE GAME: Who killed downtown St. Joseph? Was it Bill Grace by the river at the St. Jo Frontier Casino with a slot machine? Was it Patt Lilly in the St. Joseph Area Chamber of Commerce with horse blinders? Was it the whole Downtown Association in City Hall with inactivity?

KANSAS CITY CHIEFS PRACTICE BUBBLE: Kids, here is a chance to use your imagination. How many uses can you come up with for the Chiefs practice facility bubble if they decide to move their training camp to Missouri Western? How about a year-round farmers' market? What about a year-round Trails West! festival? A huge garage sale might work, too. Only your imagination and the seven controlling families of St. Joseph limit the possibilities.

December 17, 2003

Come one, come all, St. Joe kiddies big and small! It's time once again to look at all the goodies in the Alonzo Weston Catalog of Fictitious St. Joseph Toys.

We've made a list and checked it twice. We don't care about who's been naughty or who's nice. That's the business of Santa Claus and the prosecuting attorney.

Our Christmas list is pulled right from the pages of our own friendly neighborhood newspaper. And we have all sorts of goodies and surprises.

Martha Stewart is out this year, so instead we bring you the Amy Stewart and Carmento Floyd hottest items. The wives of the Missouri University associate athletic director and UM systems president respectively have just the right items for the special racially insensitive person on everybody's shopping list.

We even go across seas to bring you the newest Saddam Hussein item. And right here, from our very own Joetown artisans, we bring you some of the most controversial items ever placed on a city ballot.

Keep in mind that when I say fictional toys, I mean nonexistent. That means you'll find them in the same aisle where they keep the common courtesy.

So relax and enjoy. Keep your sense of humor and try to have a little fun this holiday season. Don't fight over toys or parking places. Don't drink and drive.

And don't worry if you're not on my list this year. Maybe you'll make it next year or maybe not. Let's see what the must-have items are this Christmas. Happy shopping:

THE LIBRARY BOARD FAMILY FEUD GAME: And the survey says the public doesn't want two libraries built within one mile of each other is the number one answer! Norma Bagnall and Marge Minor co-host this zany, wacky board game where Rolling Hills and St. Joseph Public teams compete head-to-head, trying to figure out what the reading public wants.

SADDAM'S SPIDER HOLE KIT FOR MEN: Can't find a secret place to eat those candy bars or drink that extra six-pack? The former Iraqi dictator himself endorses this complete do-it-yourself hole in the ground hideaway. Kit comes complete with shaving kit and motion detector.

"PINK TOES," THE DELTA DELTA DOLL: Just what little Ricky demons wanted to find under his tree this Christmas. Pull the string on this ivory doll and she won't talk to any college official. "Pink Toes" easily fits underneath a jail cot, discreetly out of sight of meddling college president's wives.

CARMENTO FLOYD, AMY STEWART AND RICKY CLEMONS 3-WAY WALKIE-TALKIE SET: Getting tired of those jail officials getting in your bidness? Have backstabbing, racially divisive conversations the way they were meant to be: in private. Comes in black and white models.

TRASH HAULER RISK BOARD GAME: Franchise trash service has taken over your town! Will you be the master trash hauler who achieves city dominance? Game comes with easy-to-fill-out petitions and bid sheets. Mayor David Jones and independent trash hauler Tommy Fanning game pieces not included.

SHOPPES OF NORTH VILLAGE CONSTRUX: Wanna build a Home Depot? How about an Old Navy store? All the pieces are here. Instructions cost an extra $5 million dollars.

UTILITY RATE BINGO: See who wins the next utility rate increase. Better call bingo before all the money is gone.

December 3, 2014

I never understood how people so full of turkey could be so full of fight when they go shopping on Thanksgiving Day. I'm too full of food and football to go fistfight with anybody over an Xbox One.

If anything, I'll wait until the must-have Christmas items wind up in the pawnshop a month later. Call it buzzard shopping if you want, but I'm counting my change just like the next guy. In fact, if I could get away with it, I would have Christmas a day after Christmas when everything is half price.

I once worked with a guy we called "Dirty Dave" who did just that. "Dirty Dave" was so tight, he once took a date out to dinner at a convenience store. He offered her microwave burritos for dinner. True story.

I'm not that cheap. I don't even venture out in the early morning cold for Black Friday. I'm not in that big a hurry to go spend money on more stuff.

Actually, there are no bargains to be had on Black Friday. It's just the illusion you're getting a good deal. According to a recent article in The Wall Street Journal, the best deals don't happen on Black Friday.

The Wall Street Journal had a consumer-price research firm called Decide Inc. analyze data that basically showed some items actually got much cheaper toward the end of the holiday shopping season. In fact, the study showed that some prices are even lowest way earlier in the shopping season.

Want that big-screen TV? Buy it in October. Ugg Boots? October.

Same goes for toys, according to Decide's data. The price of a Sesame Street Elmo plush toy increased 31 percent on Black Friday from its usual price.

But ya'll can rest assured there will be no price gouging here.

Shop through that community-minded, civic-dutied compendium of Christmas shopping—"The Alonzo Weston Catalog of Entirely Fictitious St. Joseph Toys"—and get a real bargain.

Remember, these toys are entirely fictional. They're all in fun, so please no lawsuits. Ease up a little and let's have some fun. Happy shopping.

MOSAIC LIFE CARE WHEEL OF FORTUNE GAME: No matter how many vowels you buy, the words still spell out Heartland Health. Contestants try to guess hidden costs by spinning a huge wheel. Careful, you can land on "bankrupt" if you don't have enough money to even afford a vowel.

SOUTH ST. JOSEPH PROGRESSIVE ASSOCIATION EASY MONEY GAME: Each player gets $3.5 million in CIP funds to purchase and develop property on a game board. Player with the best development plan wins.

THE SPANKY O'DELL DRIVER'S LICENSE VIDEO GAME: Use the mouse to maneuver your vehicle down winding city streets while dodging police. The key is to make it home before getting pulled over. Points deducted for not using your turn signal.

LARRY TOURANGEAU SCRABBLE: See how many offensive phrases against local city officials you can create by using the most cuss words. Comes with metal sign construction kit.

ST. JOSEPH SCHOOL DISTRICT CLUE BOARD GAME: Sorry, game is a work in progress. Still seeking clues.

ST. JOSEPH SMOKING ORDINANCE DOLL: Pull the string and hear the doll cough out 12 different sayings: "It's just like Nazi Germany." "Where are my rights?" "I pay taxes." "I just won't ever go out again in my life." Comes with free pack of cigarettes and 25 percent off coupon for pulmonary test.

DR. BOB VARTABEDIAN'S WALTER CRONKITE DOLLHOUSE: Comes with news set and action figures of major 20th century newsmakers. Only available in St. Joseph.

ELLIS CROSS DON'T-BLOW-YOUR-TOP GAME: "Careful, careful, you never know the one you add may make it blow." Spin the spinner and see how many charges you can add to the top of Mr. Cross' hat before the balloon on top blows. Comes with courtroom play board.

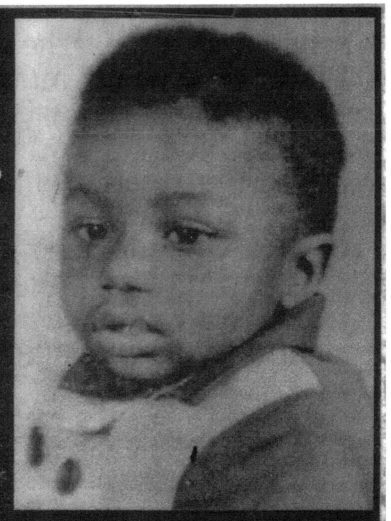

LOOK AT THIS **babyface**

Alonzo Weston

Columnist, St. Joseph News-Press

Alonzo's mother, Florestine Turner

Alonzo's biological father, Alex Wilkinson, Army

Alonzo's stepfather, Henry Turner, Sr.

Alonzo's stepfather, Henry Turner, Sr.

Alonzo's Uncle Phil King and the Phil King's Dynatones
Photo courtesy of St. Joseph Museums, Inc.

Alonzo's grandmother, Lena Weston

Lena Weston at Katz Drugstore

Lena Weston and Friends

Alonzo's Uncle PeeWee, Charles Weston

Deanna and Alonzo

Alonzo, Jr. and Nicole

Nicole Hughes

Alonzo with grandchildren Asia and Jace and dog Eubie

Alonzo, Jr.

Alonzo downtown St. Joseph, 1972

Alonzo, Central High School Track, 1972

Angie Rittman, Artie Belle King, Norman Hart, Joyce Hart, Chris McGaughy, and Alonzo, 1961

Kevin Banks, Orville Hunter, Joe Henderson, Alonzo, and Doug Vaughn

Girl's Basketball Team

Cheer Leaders

Horace Mann School Photos

Black YMCA before it became Teen Town

Ms. Black St. Joe Pageant, 1971

Alonzo with Mrs. Helen Cronkite and Bob Alcorn

Alonzo, Clarence Wilson, and John Seigenthaler press secretary to Robert Kennedy

SOMEBODY'S GOTTA SAY IT

Let's rise above hatred

I never met the Reverend Fred Phelps. But I've interviewed a few of the Westboro Baptist Church pastor's family members whenever they came to town on his behalf to protest a soldier's funeral or some other event they felt promoted homosexuality.

They proclaimed to come as messengers of God. But I've never heard of God using the language of an online troll.

"God Hates Fags" and "Thank God for Dead Soldiers" read more like bathroom wall scripture.

I dodged both spit and anger when I interviewed his daughter. It was like interviewing a rabid dog on a chain.

But this woman was off the chain. Her anger and venom flowed free and unchecked. With anger like that, I didn't know what she was capable of doing. Thank God the cops were nearby and watching.

I never like what the Phelps clan does, but I strongly support their First Amendment rights. My job depends on it. In fact, I even studied at the First Amendment Center in Nashville. However, for a moment, this hatred made me question my First Amendment loyalty.

What made it worse is that the Phelps group always brought young kids along with them. Kids too young to know the difference between mother's milk and mother's hatred. For them, it was the same.

Reverend Phelps himself never showed up at the St. Joe protests I covered. His spirit was surely there. Hatred for all things homosexual, real or perceived, passed down like a family tradition.

Hatred and intolerance blessed only by how Reverend Fred read the Bible. The labyrinthine way he detected any support for gays made everyone and everything suspect.

Soldiers dying for America were dying for a country that supported gay rights, according to the Book of Fred. Even businesses that had gay administrators were under his damnation.

His credo and the placards his family members carried at protests read "God Hates Fags." Until all vestiges of that ultimate sin were cast away, Reverend Fred wasn't going away.

But Reverend Fred might be on his way out now. Several news reports say the anti-gay pastor is "on the edge of death." He's supposedly living, or more appropriately dying, in a hospice care facility somewhere in Topeka.

His estranged son Nate Phelps told news sources that Westboro church members already had voted his dad out of his church a while back. However, that news wasn't confirmed.

By the time you read this, Reverend Fred could be dead. And the knee-jerk reaction to news of his death would signal the call for some to band together and protest at his funeral. Let his family experience the pain he's caused to others. Give them the sort of justice bad guys in the movies get and deserve. Karma is a... well, you know.

But hate never wins against hate. It's always a draw. No one hate is better than the other. It's love that always wins out.

Protesting Reverend Phelps' funeral makes us no better.

On Sunday, a Kansas gay rights group made a prepared statement to the media urging the public to support the privacy of the Phelps family. They didn't want any retaliation.

Thomas Witt, executive director of Equality Kansas, said in the statement that it was time for the community to rise above the sorrow and anger Reverend Phelps sowed.

"...show the world we are a caring and compassionate people who respect the privacy and dignity of all," Witt said.

Reverend Phelps had the volume turned up on his intolerance. But as long as we carry some sort of hatred and intolerance in own our hearts, we shouldn't even think about picking up any stones.

Anti-Christmas America

While driving through the Shoppes at North Village the other day, I couldn't find a Christmas sign to save my soul. Oh sure, there were plenty of holiday season decorations. Wreaths. Red bows. Decorated trees and holly. But I didn't see one sign or ad that said Christmas sale or anything with Christmas or Christ in it.

It was the same thing at Wal-Mart. I saw plenty of green and red colors. Some really neat toys, evergreen trees and a sign that said something about the holidays.

But I saw no Christmas.

The only store sign I saw that said anything about Christmas was at Santa's Fun Land in the East Hills Shopping Center. Above the entrance to Santa's lair, hung a big white banner that read, "Merry Christmas from the East Hills Merchants."

I know where many Christians are going to be shopping this holiday season: wherever there's the best sale.

There's an e-mail petition circulating around the Internet asking anyone who considers himself or herself a Christian to sign in protest of retailers that don't use Christmas in their promotions.

Supposedly the e-mail comes from the Reverend Donald Wildmon, founder and chairman of the American Family Association (AFA).

According to the AFA Web site, the Reverend Wildmon is an ordained Methodist minister. He founded the nonprofit organization in 1977 as a response to what he felt was an erosion of values in our society.

The AFA mission statement says that it is an organization that "exists to motivate and equip citizens to change the culture to reflect Biblical truth."

In the e-mail petition, the Reverend Wildmon concedes that it's too late to do anything about the sacrilege of banning the use of Christmas this year. But by signing the petition now, good Christians are "letting these companies know that banning 'Christmas' in their promotions and advertising next year will result in a loss of business."

The e-mail ends with a postscript from Bill O'Reilly of The O'Reilly Factor fame. "There is an anti-Christian bias in this country and it's more on display at Christmas season than at any other time," Mr. O'Reilly said.

Since its beginning, the primary focus of AFA has been television and other forms of media. They see it as their duty to take the media to task for their part in the erosion of family values. Part of that vision now includes holding companies and retailers accountable for the roles they play in the decline of society.

And for some reason, the AFA has it in its mind that leaving Christmas out of the annual holiday season shopping carnage is somehow un-Christian. True Christians should be outraged that all that pushing, shoving, rudeness and crass holiday commercialism doesn't take place under the banner of Christ.

What would Jesus do? Well, I don't think he'd call it Christmas either.

Let's call it what it is. It's holiday shopping. There's nothing Christian or holy about it.

I've never seen anyone celebrate the true meaning of Christmas in a mall.

Praying that a store has that special toy that your son wants doesn't count, either.

If it truly is about the Christ-like spirit of giving, then everyone should be fighting over who gets to put money in the Salvation Army kettle first instead of trying to get that new toy.

Think about it. Would you rather have the Christmas spirit in a store ad or in your heart? It's inside us where we truly celebrate the spirit of giving, thanksgiving and forgiving.

The importance of finding your own truth

Michelle Obama has been pretty quiet about the challenges she faces being the first African-American first lady. Both she and President Barack Obama are held to different standards and scrutiny than other presidents and first ladies. And yes, a whole lot of it has to do with race.

In today's climate, the only ones allowed to talk about race are the online trolls and people who pass along hateful racist memes about the president and the first lady in e-mails and Facebook posts. By some pretzel logic, if anyone calls them on it, they end up somehow being the racist.

When Mrs. Obama gave a speech at Tuskegee University recently and spoke of the trials she faced as both as an African-American woman and the first African-American first lady, the critics came out. She was called a race-baiter and accused of dividing the nation.

Conservative talk show host Rush Limbaugh accused her of "playing the race card." He said that he had long believed that the president and first lady are responsible for the racial divide in the country. Mr. Limbaugh even went as far as to say Mrs. Obama lied about the slights she endured.

"She's too well known—it's absurd," Mr. Limbaugh said, according to a New York Daily News article. "But she wants it to be believed. And maybe in her mind she has been treated that way by some of these people around the world she's met. Maybe she hasn't and just thought she would be, or maybe they didn't fawn enough and that's why, so she's telling herself stories about what they think of her."

Mr. Limbaugh got an amen from like-minded conservatives online and offline.

Mrs. Obama told the students about being called "Obama's baby mama" and her husband's "crony of color" on FOX News. She spoke of the New Yorker cover that depicted her wearing a huge Afro and holding a machine gun.

During the 2008 campaign, Mrs. Obama talked of the anxiety and sleepless nights worrying about what people thought of her. She feared the attacks on her husband and her family as well. Even today, people question his citizenship, she said.

"As potentially the first African-American first lady, I was also the focus of another set of questions and speculations, conversations sometimes rooted in the fears and misperceptions of others," she said, according to a CNN article.

She told the Tuskegee class of 2015 that she ultimately had to learn to focus on her own truth. The students would have to do the same when confronting racism that still exists in this country. Yet that is never an excuse to give up.

"At the end of the day, by staying true to the me I've always known, I found that this journey has been incredibly freeing. Because no matter what happened, I had the peace of mind of knowing that all of the chatter, the name calling, the doubting—all of it was just noise. It did not define me. It didn't change who I was. And most importantly, it couldn't hold me back," she said.

We live in a nation that could elect an African-American president. And it's a different world from 50 years ago, when legislation was passed that prohibited African-Americans from having the right to even vote.

In 1965, a biracial person like President Obama was thought of as a tragic figure because of his mixed heritage. Mixed marriages were still taboo.

Yet sadly today, some of those old hates and prejudices still exist. Some say they don't like some of President Obama's executive decisions but then punctuate it with racial derision or hate.

Being the first minority in any arena can be a challenge. We still have a ways to go when we have the first African-American or first Latin-American or first Native American anything.

Zimmerman verdict perplexes

My grandson Jace is scheduled to be born in a little over a month. At some point beyond his coming into the world, Jace will sit on my knee and ask questions about the life around him.

He'll ask cute little things at first, like what a butterfly is and how birds fly. Of course, he'll ask his father these things before he'll ask Grandpa. But at some point, he'll be old enough to ask questions on how to conduct himself as a man, as well as how to carry himself as a black youth and as a black man.

It saddens me that he still needs to hear this latter lesson, too.

Jace will come into a world that's in many ways different from the one I was born into. He'll know nothing of civil rights struggles, segregated schools, busing and seeing no one who looks like himself in public office or on TV. For him, our first black president will be a history lesson.

I thought of all this after watching the jury verdict Saturday night that found neighborhood watch captain George Zimmerman not guilty in the February 2012 shooting of Trayvon Martin, an unarmed black teen.

Zimmerman was told not to follow the teen, whose father lived in the Sanford, Florida gated community, but he did so anyway. Martin was on the phone with a friend, telling her he was being followed by a "creepy-ass cracker."

I wouldn't have used those words if it were me being followed. But you can bet it would have been something unfit for a family newspaper. There aren't any polite terms in describing a stalker.

What happened next is known only to Zimmerman and Martin.

Martin is dead. Dead men tell no tales. Live ones do. And Zimmerman said he shot and killed Martin in self-defense, even though he was armed and Martin was not.

Zimmerman also said Martin's last words after being shot were "you got me."

No one says "you got me" after being shot unless they're in a 1940s gangster movie. If I get shot, I'm either screaming for help or hollering, "oh (expletive deleted)."

Some people said Martin should have run after he knew he was being followed. But for some like Zimmerman, just being black in that neighborhood was an admission of guilt. Running while black would confirm it.

I've said before that I thought this case was a matter of perception instead of one about race. Martin's parents believed that, too. But I amend that statement to say it's a perception about someone's race.

When Zimmerman called police as he watched Martin walk through the neighborhood, he said, "(expletive) punks. These assholes. They always get away."

Who are "they?"

Now, after the Trayvon Martin case, I'm not sure how I'll tell my grandson how to conduct himself when he is being followed by an armed adult.

Running is not the answer. Confronting your stalker isn't an option, and sometimes calling the police isn't either. The police were on the phone that night.

However, I still believe in our legal system. I think we have the best the world has to offer. But it's also one in which winning a case doesn't always guarantee the truth. Just look at O. J. or Casey Anthony.

By the time Jace asks what he can expect of being a black male, I hope I can tell him about better things than what we still see happen today. But today, being a black male in this society means you still run the greater risk of being killed by someone who looks like you than someone who doesn't like how you look.

Smile of innocence can fade over time

My grandson Jace Michael is a happy boy. He's a pretty boy, too. I know that not just from being his grandpa, but everyone tells me that, too. His smile is one of pure joy. Only 14 months in the world, Jace Michael has only seen the love the world has to offer. He smiles. People smile back. He cries. Everyone tends to his needs.

Jace Michael's namesake, Shawn Michael, had a smile like that. Shawn Michael was my cousin who my wife and I sort of adopted as our own. He went to baseball games, movies, celebrated birthdays with us just like our own kids.

Shawn Michael was an innocent sweet kid too. His smile was untainted by the troubles and prejudices of the world.

Shawn was a black male too. Somewhere along the way, things changed. No longer was he the cute adorable young boy who made everyone smile but was perceived as a threat to some segments to society. Instead of smiles, he got looks of suspicion.

He would face racism and be told to act a certain way. He might have been told that to be authentically black he would have to adopt a certain stance. He no doubt saw other black males like himself getting killed at the hands of other black males and the police.

He saw and experienced things all black males including myself go through at one time or another.

All this can change a youthful, innocent smile.

Shawn got killed three years ago at the hands of another black male. Whether by the police or another black male, the life of a black male seems worthless. Somewhere along the way, our young black males lose their sense of self-worth, whether by people who look like themselves or society as a whole.

The shooting death of 18-year-old Michael Brown in Ferguson Missouri, and the grand jury decision to not indict police officer Darren Wilson for his shooting death seems like yet another reminder how much less valuable black males seem to be.

It brings back not long ago memories of Trayvon Martin, who in 2012 was fatally shot by George Zimmerman, a neighborhood watch volunteer in a gated Miami community. Zimmerman too was not convicted of shooting the unarmed teen.

After the grand jury in Ferguson announced its decision Monday night, protests were staged all over the country as a result. Buildings burned and more than 60 people were arrested in Ferguson as a result of racially charged rioting.

Even after the grand jury verdict, there are still lots of unanswered questions. The teen was unarmed, even running away at one point.

Chad Dion Lassiter is a nationally recognized expert on American race relations and violence prevention among African-American males, who seeks to recruit black males into the profession of social work and provide anti-racism and violence prevention.

He is co-founder and president of the Black Men at Penn School of Social Work at the University of Pennsylvania. In an e-mail response, he said the grand jury failed to present a coherent narrative that explained Wilson's behavior. He said the criminal justice system continues to protect whiteness at the cost of dead black bodies.

"With impunity and the question now is can you stop the killing of unarmed black males or is your irrational hatred toward black folks deeply rooted in your psyche and DNA? I am ashamed of the criminal justice system but not surprised at the outcome of the verdict. W.E.B. Dubois stated that a system cannot fail those it was never built to protect.

In the face of all this there are those who continue to say we shouldn't talk about race. There are those who claim they don't see race. Incidents like in Ferguson show we can't ignore race is a problem in America.

I will do everything in my power to see that my grandson Jace Michael does not lose that smile lost by Shawn Michael and so many other young black males. My job and that of others is to make sure these youths see their worth regardless of what anyone else thinks.

Drunken Mary, Crazy Roger

We never bothered with knowing their last names. She was just "Drunken Mary." He was simply "Crazy Roger."

One we dreaded to see coming. The other we were delighted to see for all the wrong reasons.

From four blocks away, we could tell it was Drunken Mary. She looked just like the Mummy, dragging her left leg and holding her tattered overcoat closed with one hand as she limped her way up the sidewalk to Jake's Drug Store. Early every day she made the trip to get her "medicine."

I always tried to hide until she was well past our house.

I knew that if she caught me, she'd plant a slobbery kiss on my cheek that always reeked of cheap, stale wine.

But as much as we dreaded seeing Drunken Mary, we couldn't wait to see Crazy Roger. If we missed him, we missed a good laugh. We might miss seeing him walk up the street with his pants off. We could miss hearing him carry on a conversation and argue with himself.

All of us kids feared Mary. And we all saw Roger as a novelty. We didn't know any better. Perhaps neither did anyone else.

For many people then and now, fear and ridicule are the only two ways to look at mental illness.

It wasn't until years later that I learned the truth. Mary, I learned, tried to self-medicate her mental illness with alcohol. Way too late to apologize, I found out that Roger suffered from schizophrenia, an ailment not any different from diabetes or lupus. The only difference was that his illness affected his mind.

This type of education is the whole reason behind Mental Health Awareness Month. Every October, the American Psychiatric Association and other mental-health entities try to clear up misconceptions and address the problems of mental illness.

It may not affect some of us directly, but it could or maybe does affect someone in our family or an acquaintance. It could be anyone of us too, as depression and anxiety have become more prevalent in our society.

Prozac, Paxil and other anti-depression drugs are some of the most prescribed medicines today. Yet many people think mental illness is a character flaw or a sign of weakness.

According to a survey reported on the Mind Publications Web site, 70 percent of people think the cause of mental illness is a personal weakness. It's reported also that these 7 out of 10 people who subscribe to this theory think that if a person would just try harder, they could overcome mental illness.

People suffering from a mental or emotional disorder are often labeled lazy of crazy. Wives and husbands have left their spouses because the other suffers from a mental illness. Yet at the same time, those same people would most likely stand by them if they suffered a stroke or other malady.

This same view of mental illness also is found on a much larger level. Mental-health care is usually on the rung of lowest priority when it comes to state and federal funding. Because of this, many people can't get the proper care they need simply to live.

As a result, they're either locked up or thrown out onto the street, homeless and without a chance, because their care providers couldn't provide services because of budget cuts.

Funny how things have a way of coming back around.

Along time ago, I laughed and ran away from people like Mary and Roger.

Now, part of my job is to cover mental health for this newspaper. And being on this beat, I've run across a few more Marys and Rogers. Good people. People who only want hope and understanding.

That was all Mary and Roger ever wanted: that and the small dignity of a last name.

How will smoking ban affect mentally ill?

Tina (not her real name) needed cigarettes like she needed a loaf of bread and a gallon of milk. The cigarettes, she said, kept her anxiety at bay. Without her cigarettes, Tina would be a nervous wreck.

Ordinarily, I don't buy anyone alcohol or cigarettes. But I've covered the mental health field long enough to know that persons suffering from mental illnesses seem to smoke more than the general population. The Centers for Disease Control and Prevention (CDC) have data to back up that assertion.

According to a 2011 study on the CDC website, adults with some form of mental illness have a smoking rate 70 percent higher than adults with no mental illness. The report showed that 36 percent of adults with mental illness are cigarette smokers compared with 21 percent of adults who have no mental illness.

While covering the mental health beat, I often had to go to the Peace of Mind center, a recreational facility for the mentally ill. The place was as smoky as the old city auditorium during Friday night wrestling matches.

In fact, the smoke was so bad at Peace of Mind it caused problems with its next-door neighboring business. When Peace of Mind moved next door to the Youth Alliance offices when it was on Francis Street, Youth Alliance officials claimed that the smoke created a health hazard for its employees. The owner of the facility at the time said he wouldn't spend the money to make the place smoke-free. If they wanted, the tenants could move, he said.

That was in 2005, a scant nine years ago, but in the way smoking is viewed today, it seems like eons ago. St. Joseph voters passed a smoking ban in April that bans smoking in all indoor places of employment, and it will go into effect this Saturday.

Many apartment buildings and other places also are going smoke-free. Only the St. Jo Frontier Casino's gaming floor is exempt from the ban.

I wondered what effect the ban might have on the mentally ill population. It's probably too early to tell, of course, but I wondered why those suffering from mental illness seemed to smoke more than the rest of the population.

A couple of local psychologists gave their opinions. Smoking probably has more to do with boredom than anything else, they said.

Dr. Shirley Taylor, a Heartland licensed psychologist, said she knows about the phenomenon from experience, not research. Dr. Taylor said when she worked at the St. Louis state hospital, almost everyone smoked.

"It was a way to connect with somebody else; you go out and smoke together, there was nothing else for them to do so there was a boredom factor and I think it's probably when you're in that sort of ritual, it relieves some anxiety," she said.

Kenneth Hines, another local psychologist, said if you mean "mentally ill" to be those who are hospitalized or disabled in sheltered care, then it probably has to do with boredom.

"Alcoholics in treatment do the same thing; so do prisoners, if they have easy access to cigarettes and coffee," he said.

But the mentally ill who are in the regular population more often match the rest of the population when it comes to smoking, Mr. Hines said.

"People with too much time on their hands are more susceptible to boredom and smoking, etc., followed closely by addictive behaviors of all sorts, including digital gaming, porn-surfing, texting, etc. The connection is probably indirect," he said.

St Joseph Memes is all right with me

Whenever some of my friends and I get together, a passer-by would think that we hated each other after listening to one of our conversations. They can get down and dirty sometimes.

We have no boundaries. It could get racial. It could be about somebody's momma. It could be whatever it takes to get the upper hand.

I worked in a factory for a number of years, and one of the things you learned quick was that you'd better have thick skin. Guys go out of their way to find your weakness. The key is to not get mad, but give it right back.

Even conversations here at the newspaper between Steve Booher, Ken Newton, Ross Martin, Ray Scherer, Terry Jordan and me might seem insulting to an outsider. But it's taken in the spirit of friendship. No offense is taken.

That's sort of the way I look at the Facebook page, St. Joe Memes. People either love or hate the site that pokes fun at people and things unique to St. Joseph.

I'm not friends with Cody Hall and Boston Archer, the site's creators, but I never pass up a chance to experience some satire. Heck, I even try to get away with some in my column.

St. Joe Memes first came to my attention after someone alerted me to a post on the site from someone asking if anyone had the guts to make a meme of the "race-baiting" racist Alonzo Weston.

I found out the person requesting the meme didn't give his or her true identity. But that's nothing new to me. I'm a seasoned veteran of the online comments and "It's your call" vitriol. I'm used to being called a race-baiter, racist and everything short of a cat killer in those forums. They get no fresh meat here.

146

Since no one had the guts or the desire to make an insulting meme of me, I decided to make one myself. With the help of my News-Press colleague Clinton Thomas, we created a meme from an old photo in my Facebook files, of me ringing a Salvation Army bell.

The caption read: "Alonzo Weston: always looking for a handout."

A few people, including one of the St. Joe Memes site administrators, thought it was a hilarious idea. I had a choice to either get mad or play along. By making fun of myself, it defused the anger of the situation.

And that was easy. I've never had any qualms about making fun of myself. I'm not perfect and I know it. Ask my wife.

I live in St. Joseph, too, and I'll defend its virtues to any outsider. We have beautiful old homes and architecture. We have friendly people and good schools. It's truly a good place to live.

If I were in a witness protection program, I'd choose to live here.

But there's the other side, too. We have people who think that pajama bottoms and flip-flops are proper courtroom attire. We have people eating hot dogs at a drug bust like it's a sporting event.

We had a mayor who slapped a woman in the face with a steak. We've had cops arresting people for having plastic skeletons hanging from their rear-view mirrors.

Several years back, an e-mail circulated around that said "You know you are a native of St. Joseph, Missouri if…"

It had entries like "Your lifetime goal is to own a fireworks stand" and "You've ever barbecued Spam on a grill."

Getting upset about St. Joseph Memes makes us look like the snooty old matriarch who would never admit to ever having passed gas.

Of course, satire does have boundaries. It's very easy to cross the line into outright hatefulness. That should never be the intent.

But sometimes we need to laugh at ourselves. It's what family and friends do to each other.

Wives

If I left work on time, I'd see Joe. He'd be limping fast up Ninth Street, trying to get home to an empty house before dark. I'd always offer him a ride.

Joe would always say thanks before he let out a tired sigh and plopped himself down in the passenger seat. The conversation would always begin with him telling me how the trip was wearing him out. His legs were swollen and sore every night when he got home, he said.

If he didn't get a ride, it was a four-mile round trip every day walking from his home in midtown to a downtown care center. He'd leave early in the morning and stay all day. That was exhausting too, but he did it because he needed to, he said. And of course he did it because he wanted to see his wife.

It didn't matter that she was dying of brain cancer and didn't remember who he was now. Thank God she slept most of the time. Waking moments were sometimes filled with screams of pain or moans. Just being able to hold her hand was good enough now. Before long he'd just have to hold her in his heart.

A few times after giving Joe a ride, I'd come home to an empty house. My wife would not be there. She would either be picking up something for supper, working late or out at the mall. No big deal.

Except for one time.

One particular evening after dropping Joe off, I came home to find not a single light on in the house. Just the evening light shining through the windows. And it seemed to cast a bluish gray loneliness all over everything in the living room.

I stood still for a while. Listening. Waiting to hear footsteps upstairs or in the kitchen. My wife's voice. Anything, but nothing. Nothing except the somnambulant hum of the refrigerator and the impassive, single-minded ticks of the dining room clock. It occurred to me that this is how it would be every night if my wife weren't here. This is how it is for Joe every night now.

Maybe that's how the last 15 years have been for Michael Schiavo. His wife Terri lying in a "persistent vegetative state," the doctor's words, in a hospital bed. "Persistent vegetative state" means she can follow things with her eyes. It means she can smile sometimes. It also means she lives with a feeding tube. Michael Schiavo didn't get any instructions from his wife on how long he should hold on. All the vows said were, "until death do us part." They never said what death was.

Mr. Schiavo believed death happened long ago. He wanted the feeding tube that's keeping his wife alive removed. The United States Congress believes it knows what death means too. And it passed a measure to go against Mr. Schiavo's wishes to keep his wife alive.

Protesters outside the Florida hospice where Terri Schiavo stays hold signs saying to keep her alive, too. But what do they know?

Who are they to make any decision? It's not even Terri's parents' decision. Isn't that covered in the marriage vows too?

No protesters, no senators and no parents had to tell Joe how long he should stay. He just listened to his heart. After a while I started trying to leave work on time so I could give Joe a ride home. A lot of times I didn't make it. But then I didn't see Joe for a while either.

When I finally did see him it was right before Christmas. Right after his wife had died. His legs felt better, he said. But not much gets him out of a lonely house these days.

Sometimes in the evenings, my wife and I sit quietly in our living room, she on the couch, me in the recliner. We don't always speak much. Some times it's a few words here and there. At other times it's a nod, a look or a smile. We've been together long enough that we can know what each other is thinking and feeling without talking. We just know.

Dress Code

Used to be if you hadn't been to church in a while, you needed a new suit to get back in. For many of us that meant you had to wait until Easter. Back in the day, that was the only time anyone ever got any new dress clothes.

Now I don't know who thought up the rule that you had to be dressed up to go to church. After all, Jesus just wore a robe and sandals everywhere, the same attire that got Ray Charles Jones kicked out of 12th-grade English class, as I remember.

The only way a new suit in church might get you into heaven is if you're wearing it to your funeral. Other than that, you're just joining the fashion show of Sunday morning sinners.

And that's all church is for some: a fashion show. Some folks will tell you that getting dressed up is their way of showing honor to the Lord. But for some churchwomen, that benevolence only lasted until someone else showed up wearing the same prayer.

Nevertheless, suits and ties for men and dresses for women were mandatory church attire in the past. And it wasn't just at church where you had to get dressed up. You had to get decked out and spit-shined for job interviews, weddings, office jobs and dates. That's how it used to be.

Fast forward to today, where if you're caught wearing a new suit to church, it means you haven't been in awhile. And I mean for a long while.

Most people stopped getting dressed up to go to church, or anywhere else for that matter, a long time ago. Jean shorts and flip-flops are the sartorial doctrine for the masses today.

We've become a dress-casual society. And our new anthem is "don't worry, be casual."

This past Sunday, we ran a Chicago Tribune editorial in our paper about the Northwestern University women's lacrosse team showing up at the White House in flip-flop sandals. What justified that fashion gaffe, the article said, was the fact that the women were wearing the sandals for a noble cause. The article said they were wearing them to promote a flip-flop auction to help raise money for a 10-year-old girl suffering from a brain tumor.

But to me, just the thought that someone actually was willing to bid money, no matter what the cause, for these symbols of our casualness says something about our culture. But I'm not sure what. Maybe all it says is that we value our right to dress down. Or maybe it says after working 80-hour weeks to pay off our monumental credit card debt that we have to get some semblance of leisure in where we can.

No one knew what casual Fridays were when I first came to work at the newspaper 16 years ago. No one anywhere knew what it meant.

One of the big rules here back then was that you came to work dressed in formal business attire. The rule was always enforced but within reason.

For example, no one expected you to cover a mud-a-thon in a three-piece suit.

Likewise, no one looked for you to show up at the governor's news conference wearing a Chiefs jersey and Tommy Hilfiger jean shorts.

One time on a story, I wore dress clothes while walking through heavy brush and timber, looking for a freshwater spring with some farmer. Needless to say, cockle burr sequins on double-knit slacks never became a fad.

Now, as I suspect it is in many offices, we have people coming to work wearing shorts and jeans on days other than casual Friday. Many times, it's the sports writers. Most of them are an iconoclastic breed anyway. But we also have some beat reporters and interns who come to work in flip-flops and other casual attire.

153

I see kids now going for job interviews wearing baggy T-shirts and jeans shorts well below the crack. What's even more amazing is that they get hired. Maybe it's at McDonald's, but they get hired.

I've seen salesmen in corporate offices wearing jeans and T-shirts. Once I even saw a monk wearing a NASCAR ball cap.

Ultimately, there are many more things to worry about in this world than who is or isn't getting dressed up. But sometimes it would be nice to know whether I'm in church or at a Royals baseball game.

Come to think of it, didn't people used to wear suits and ties to baseball games too?

Would you want to live forever?

My mother-in-law asked for a beer before she died. She didn't drink. But she was ready to go out with a cold one. For her, dying might be better chased down with a beer.

When the doctor told my father he could either die or undergo a procedure where the odds were so high he would probably die anyway, he said, "Damned if I do, damned if I don't, huh?"

He just closed his eyes in acceptance.

I visited a good friend a week before he died. We watched an NBA final that he would never live to see the winner. He knew that. He accepted it. When I told him I'd see him next week, his look just said goodbye.

No one knows how they will act when faced with death. I'd like to think I'll go out with dignity, maybe wearing an ascot and spouting very profound last words. But more likely, I'll be kicking and screaming, grabbing onto any earthly foundation I can find, while the specter of death drags me out of the room.

No one likes to talk about death, but everyone knows they will die someday. The younger you are, the farther away that someday seems.

I never thought much about dying until I turned 40. I drove fast, drank hard and played sports with little regard for my body or safety. Something about turning 40 made me more aware of my mortality.

Every lingering cough, back pain, stomach pain or headache became suspect.

Every time was the time I would get bad news. I waited on test results like watching rolling dice on a craps table.

Of course, I was relieved when the test results came back normal. But since 40, I've been living from blood test to blood test and X-ray to X-ray, waiting for that day when the doctor comes in the room and slowly closes the door behind him.

Last checkup, my nurse Coleen told me I was the healthiest dying man she knows. Coleen has been my nurse through two doctors and several sure signs of my death. I might as well have her on speed dial.

But as afraid as I am of death, I don't know if I'd want to live forever. Seeing history repeat itself a few times in a normal life span adds to a person's wisdom. To see reruns for eternity is like living through an endless series of Me TV. The good sitcoms and the bad ones play over and over and you can't change the channel.

But the upside to being immortal is you can do all the crazy stuff you fear to do but wanted to do, like jump out of an airplane. I'd ride roller coasters, pick fights, drink hard, drive fast and eat whatever I wanted.

Only thing is, I don't want to do all of this stuff in an old man's body. Who wants to invite a 500-year-old guy to a party and one who looks his age at that? Every conversation would sound like a history lesson.

But immortality might be possible someday, according to some researchers.

Ray Kurzweil, a Google engineer and futurist, along with a group of like-minded thinkers, formed the Immortality Project. Funded by a $5 million grant, the project will look at everything from nature to near-death experiences to religion and the environment for clues to living longer.

The group held a conference last weekend at the University of California-Riverside to explore these issues.

Questions to ponder would be, how much money do you need to live for eternity? What about over-population? What about outliving your loved ones and friends?

Some days, death doesn't sound so bad. I heard heaven described once as one continuous loop of a person's best earthly experiences. I can live with that.

Scary stuff: Ghosts, goblins and hospital bills

Just in time for Halloween, I have a hospital billing story. Anyone who has had to deal with the Heartland/Mosaic hospital billing system knows that it is a story that will make your hair stand on end.

If it was a movie, the audience would scream "don't open it!" when you approached your mailbox. The bills inside would attack you with a vengeance.

Mosaic is a fitting addition to the Heartland name. You don't get just one hospital bill, you get a mosaic of charges. There's the radiologist, the physician, the butcher, baker and the candlestick maker.

Before I go any further let me say this: I think Heartland/Mosaic for the most part is a fine hospital. The doctors who helped me during my back surgery were top shelf. And, I'd put our nurses at Heartland up against the ones at any other hospital. They're caring and they go the extra mile.

There are nice people in billing too, but they're working for a monster of a system that they didn't create. Nevertheless, they're the ones who have to deal with the pitchforks and torches of angry clients.

The emergency room has its issues, too.

My Heartland horror experience began when I had back problems last year. Everything leading up to my surgery was fine. The staff and doctors were exemplars of competency.

Problems began the day of my surgery. I was scheduled for surgery early that Monday morning. I was put to sleep, only to be awakened soon after because they couldn't read the radiologist's disk. They finally got a readable disk, and I had to be put back to sleep.

Things went well until that following Friday, when I woke up in excruciating pain—so much that my wife had to call an ambulance to take me to the hospital.

Now, I have never been in an ambulance in my life. I didn't even call one when I got stabbed in the back during a fight when I was 18. I drove myself to the hospital.

But when I got to the emergency room, the ER doctor was going to send me right back home. That's when my wife went into pit bull mode. She said I came out in an ambulance and I wasn't leaving until I was seen by my doctor. I ended up staying in the hospital for the weekend, so full of painkillers I felt like a zombie.

The real horror came when I started getting bills. I went to Heartland billing, where one lady was nice enough to sit down and go over the bills with me. She saw some discrepancies and said she would look into the problems. A few weeks later she told me what was paid and what I owed. I paid what I owed and thought I was done with it. I called the office and talked to another lady later and asked her "Are you sure that's all I owe?"

She said I had another bill, from Northwest Financial Services, for the pain clinic. Northwest called me and said I owed the money, too.

Then, about a month ago, I got three refund checks totaling about $75, saying I overpaid the pain clinic. I spoke to Northwest and Heartland again, asking how I could have a refund and still owe money.

I got some convoluted answer. I admit I got nasty. When I paid Northwest, I asked, "Is this it?"

"Right now," the lady said.

That right there told me that Heartland bills are zombies. They never die.

The problem is a billing system that's hard for the average person to decipher. How many older people do you think get confused about all the bills that come from Heartland?

159

The Affordable Care Act isn't perfect. But the state of health care as it stands now is miles away from perfect. That's what's really scary.

Do we really hate the poor? It's possible; just think about it

We watched her every move, the other people in line and I. Her bony, nicotine stained fingers resembled a fishing net repeatedly being cast into her purse. Each time, the net was emptied on the counter and sifted through. Sometimes the net would snag a stray nickel or dime but more often than not, it would yield nothing but gum wrappers, old bills and receipts.

We rolled our eyes at each other impatiently as we watched her fish and fish until her catch was big enough to satisfy the store clerk. All that work, we thought to ourselves, for a pack of cigarettes and a can of pop.

It's funny how some of us never really notice the poor until they hold up the line. According to a recent study by a University of Michigan professor, a large number of people downright hate the poor for halting the flow of progress in society.

"The poor are deeply threatening to our national character," said John Tropman, a University of Michigan sociology professor who studied public attitudes toward the disadvantaged as quoted recently in the Washington Post.

He recently published a book on the subject titled, "Does America Hate the Poor? The Other American Dilemma."

We're the land of opportunity, we're the land of hope, we're the country of choice in the world market of countries," he said. "It seems threatening to our core values to admit there's a potential downside."

A recent Washington Post survey on attitudes about the poor found that while 47 percent of the respondents felt the poor were poor because of circumstances beyond their control, 46 percent believed their plight was because of a lack of effort or some character flaw. Maybe hate is too strong a word for most people when it comes to their feelings about the poor, but more than a few of us can't help but think maybe the poor contributed to their station in life someway.

We know there are people on welfare who honestly need the assistance, such as those who lost jobs or are disabled. But our problem is we can't tell the truly needy from the "welfare queens" and others who make a career out of playing the system. It's much easier on our psyches, our stress levels or whatever, to stereotype them all as the lowest-common denominator.

Maybe the proper term for our feelings about the poor is fear. Global threats, disease, economics—the daily news has helped to make us extremely sensitive to the volatility of our lives today. We know in the back of our minds all too well that we are one layoff, one downsizing or one slip on a banana peel away from the same plight.

Sure we give to the United Way and other agencies designed to help the poor and needy because we know it could very well be us someday.

But that's where we don't have to see them or they don't get in our way. We can deal with the poor all right as long as they don't hold up the line with their penny counting, like the lady in the store.

The more I thought about her, as I watched her leave the store, the more I came to realize she was no different than the rest of us, really. She had enough that day to get her by for another—just like we all did.

Fast-food workers are people too

Most times I don't even notice the fast-food worker who serves me up the heart attack with fries. They're as faceless as the voice on the drive-through window intercom.

Even when I pull up to the window to get my order, it's an impersonal affair. I grab my sack, look inside to see if my order is right, and drive off.

Now, some say "have a nice day." I respond back with reciprocal courtesy and drive off to more important things in my day.

It's not much different when you order inside a fast-food joint. In fact, it's so easy, even a caveman can do it. You don't even have to say you want "burger, fries and a drink." You just point to a number.

The person behind the counter is just as faceless as a pop machine. You put your money down and she brings your order. That's it. No interaction.

She could pull a gun on you and you couldn't give the police a description. That's how much attention many of us pay to fast-food clerks.

But they are somebody. They are somebody's kid. More often than not anymore, they're somebody's wife, husband or mother. They're people trying to make ends meet after losing a good-paying job, or maybe their retirement money ran out.

Practically all of them make $7.25 an hour, the current federal minimum wage. That's $290, before taxes, for a 40-hour workweek.

By the time you pay rent and utilities and buy food, there's nothing left. Nothing left but survival.

They're working poor who need government assistance and free and reduced-price lunch for their children.

163

Yes, these folks can take another minimum-wage job, but what happens to their home life? If they have kids, they're more often than not left unattended.

I thought of all this after I heard about the recent strike across the country. Fast-food workers in about 60 cities went on strike or walked off their jobs. They wanted their wages doubled to $15 an hour.

"The bottom line is, we are doing this to let the corporations know we want $15 an hour, better working conditions, and we want to be treated fairly," said the Reverend W.J. Rideout III of All God's People Church in Detroit in a USA Today interview. Restaurants also closed in Milwaukee, St. Louis, Boston and other cities.

Scott DeFife, executive vice president of policy and government affairs for the National Restaurant Association, said the industry provides 13 million people in the country with jobs. Most of them earn more than the minimum wage, he told the Chicago Tribune.

"Only 5 percent of restaurant employees earn the minimum wage. Those that do are predominantly working part-time and half are teenagers," Mr. DeFife said.

Critics all over are saying these folks need to get a better job or a better education. No one owes them anything in life.

But there are many college grads now forced to take jobs in fast food or other retail services. A recent McKinsey on Society report found that about 120,000 graduates who earned bachelor's degrees last year are working in restaurants or other retail work.

Sure, there will always be people who won't work or can't pass a drug test to even get a job. But that's not the norm. There are good, hardworking people out there, trying to make ends meet with an honest day's work.

Really, let's say every one of these fast food and service workers got a better job. Who would serve us? We surely don't want any illegal aliens taking those jobs, now, do we?

Weather becoming more like modern lifestyles: instant change

You used to have to wait on the seasons. One would last long enough for you to get tired of it and you would anticipate the other.

And winter was the most stubborn. Asking it to leave and make room for spring was akin to asking your teenager to shovel the snow in the driveway to make room for your family car. Your best bet either way was just to patiently wait for it to thaw.

Spring couldn't come soon enough with its rains and fog and morels and daffodils. But then it seemed like it always took forever for summer to come and school to let out.

Too many dog days of summer, too many mosquitoes, too much talk about the heat index and we couldn't wait until autumn with its cooler temperatures and beautiful trees. And that just made us impatient for winter again, with its sleigh rides, snowball fights and Christmas trees.

Now if the seasons were children we'd have them all on Ritalin. They all squirm around and get fidgety if either is asked to stay seated for the three months required of a season.

The weather's attention span is so short now that it's possible to have all four seasons show up in one week.

Wish it were summer? Just wait a few days and it will feel like it again. Go to bed and wake up the next day and you'll wonder if Santa has come and gone. There may be six inches of snow on the ground.

No answers as to why the seasons come and go so rapidly ever seem good enough. There seems like a million reasons why and they all fall somewhere between what science tries to tell you and what every man tries to explain.

The climatologists will tell you it all has to do with El Niño, La Niña and a bunch of other heavy weather jargon you need a master's degree to decipher.

Don Seals is a God-fearing man and he will tell you it's biblical.

"They talk about the changing weather in the last days of the Bible," he said.

"I think it has something to do with the Lord coming back. And it's not only the weather but other things that are transpiring in the world."

Mr. Seals has lived in St. Joseph for all of his 60 years on earth. He can remember when it would snow so heavily the whole town would practically shut down. And the mounds of snow the snowplows would build lasted for months.

But he can't remember when if ever he had to cut your grass in March like many folks in town had to do this year.

"I can't remember seeing grass turn green in March," he said.

"I have seen it snow in April but it would be gone the next day. Temperatures are just not constant anymore."

I wonder if any of us now could stand a constant temperature and a true season?

We who can get meals from a drive through window, we who can get 200 channels, we who can get anything we want with one swipe of a credit card don't have to wait for anything.

I believe in some form or another you get what you ask for in this life.

The weather is only accommodating the life many of us have come to want, no constants and no commitments and instant gratification.

News weighs heavily on reporters

The lasting image I have of the late St. Joseph News-Press photographer Ival Lawhon is of him running through the newsroom, camera equipment jangling, on his way to shoot a fire, a wreck or some other catastrophe.

If the photos were graphically tragic, Ival kept his emotions to himself. I suspected it was because he saw worse as a Vietnam War veteran. Detached emotion served as a survival tactic.

Only when I rode with Ival on the way to cover a story would he talk about some of the horrific shots he took and scenes he saw as a photographer.

A burning skeleton of a man sitting in the driver's seat of a pickup after it had been hit by a semi and caught fire. A severed head rolling down the Belt Highway after a fatal car collision. Kids dead in a car after running into a stone cemetery wall. A man's face embedded into an I-beam after his car had crashed through the roof of a house.

Ival dealt with those tragedies in his own way. As news reporters and photographers, that's what we all have to do. One of the job requirements as news reporters and photographers is to hold your emotions in check. You're charged with being objective. Unless you write a column, your opinions don't stray from the newsroom. And even if you do write a column, it better not be on a beat or story you're covering as news.

I've been in press boxes for Chiefs games and no one cheered when the home team scored. You applaud no one but stand for the Pledge of Allegiance. You cover tragedies with as straight a face as you can muster.

Still, those things take their toll on your mental well-being. In a five-part series, The Huffington Post recognized the little-known mental health epidemic in the newsroom.

"Those covering natural disasters or war are not the only ones who suffer. It turns out that almost all journalists are exposed to traumatic-stress experiences," said Elana Newman, a professor of psychology at the University of Tulsa as quoted in the story.

Gabriel Arana, the author of the first installment, wrote that "as much as journalists may fancy themselves superhuman observers of history, the truth is that we are as susceptible to trauma as the victims whose stories we tell."

The series opens with an account of John McCusker, a New Orleans Times-Picayune reporter covering Hurricane Katrina. He too lost his home and possessions in the aftermath but still worked covering the destruction and documenting the trauma all around him.

A year later McCusker was stopped by police after being discovered driving erratically. He begged the officers to take his life.

That's just what can happen when dealing with horrible tragedies. There're lawsuits, threats, hate mail and abuse on social media. That's not to mention the standard workplace stressors such as deadlines and added workload.

"Being a journalist is more stressful than people realize," said Ms. Newman.

I've never seen bodies mangled from wrecks or other horrific tragedies, but I've talked to the people left to deal with those traumatic events.

I've sat with a father whose daughter was murdered by a fellow student and I've interviewed and broke bread with relatives of a pregnant woman who was killed when a baby was ripped from her body.

I wrote stories about the Conception Abbey shootings in 2002. I interviewed a mother whose son committed suicide because the post-traumatic stress disorder from serving in the war was too much for him to handle. I wrote about how she died a year after her son's death.

With all that, the stress of deadlines, online remarks and hate mail matters little to me. I've been called a racist and an Uncle Tom, a liberal and a conservative. I take that ambiguity as a good sign of my objectivity. Although it's not what I signed up for, it's part of the job.

Even though I haven't figured the world out, my job helps me understand it and people a little better.

BAG-HEAD JHERI THE MESSANIE ST. PHILOSOPHER

January 23,1996

I was cruising down Messanie Street one day last week when I saw this big, fat black man trying to flag me down.

He looked like an offensive lineman for the Dallas Cowboys except he had a plastic bag on his head and a trash bag full of aluminum cans on his hip. As I got closer I could tell it was none other than "Bag-Head Jheri," the Messanie Street philosopher.

"What's goin' on, Bag?" I asked as I wheeled over to the curb next to him.

"Um-Um-Um. What's the matter with you, boy? Tellin' people you wanna be white?" he said while shaking his head.

He was referring to the column I'd written last week where I said I wanted to be white for a day so as to better understand the pain and racism of reverse discrimination.

I was inspired to write about it after reading about a Seattle Times columnist who opened up a forum in his column for white men to vent their frustrations about the matter.

"I just wanted to get across the point that in order for us to better understand each other we had to trade places," I said.

"Those white boys ain't got it that bad where anyone of them would wanna trade places with us, I bet," said Bag-Head. "They get a little taste of their own medicine for a few years and wanna start cryin'. Let them go through 400 years of that crap like me then come back complainin'?"

"Bag, you're old but you're not that old. I don't know any other black person that old either," I tried to reason.

"Don't get too cute with me, boy. You know what I mean," Bag-Head snapped back. "I know none of us are that old, but the pain of racism for us has been handed down from generation to generation like an heirloom. And over the years, many of them made sure we didn't lose it either. "

"But that's not all whites. Isn't it time now for us all to bury the hatchet and learn to be fair?" I asked.

He ignored my question.

"They got nerve to be mad at us for a problem they created," he said. "I had a white man have the nerve to come up to me and ask why we had to be so separatist, like why we had black museums and black magazines and stuff. I said 'You're blaming the wrong people. If we weren't left out of your museums and magazines and history in the first place, there'd be no need for any of it.' "

"Bag, what can all of us do then to help erase racism?" I asked.

"There's too many whites out there feeling superior just because they're white and there's too many blacks out there feeling inferior because they're black," he said. "And I don't know anybody wanna trade places neither 'cept you n' Michael Jackson."

"I said I'd trade for a day," I reminded him.

"Don't ever, ever say you wanna trade places with no white man, boy" reprimanded Jheri. "You already said that some of them ain't much liking it themselves now either. We done been there."

The rain was falling pretty hard Saturday as I stepped outside the News-Press building.

I heard the rapid clank, clank, clanking of aluminum cans slamming together before I could make out the huge figure with two trash bags full of aluminum cans fastened to his belt and a plastic bag on his head.

"Hey Weston, Weston. Brutha, do I got some revelation for ya."

It was Bag-Head Jheri, the Messanie Street philosopher. What could possibly be on his mind now?

"Yeah, what is it, Bag? I want to get home before I get soaked," I said impatiently.

"Remember when I told you some time back that Bill Clinton reminded me of some brutha I knew back home in South Carolina?"

"Yeah, I still remember, unfortunately."

"Well, I hear the great poet-writer Toni Morrison was saying that black folk already have a black president and she thinks it's Bill Clinton."

"Yeah, I heard that somewhere too. Everyone has a lapse of reason every now and then," I said.

"No man, I think it's true too," said Bag, "I believe Clinton really is a brutha."

"Yeah, everyone has a lapse of reason, Bag," I repeated, "But you're on a continuous slide."

"No, man, Toni think Bill be black cause he play the sax and try to pass all these bills and start all these programs to help black folk," Bag said. "I say Kenny G plays a sax too and he white bread as they can be even if he do have a Jheri-Curl perm. He ain't the first white man in office that tried to cater to black folk either."

"Look Bag, I'm getting soaked standing out here. What's your point, man?" I asked impatiently.

"I say Bill Clinton is black just like O.J. Simpson is black," Bag said.

"Wha-a-at?" I asked incredulously.

"That's right," Bag said smugly. "Check this out: Only time O.J. wanted anything to do with black folks was when he got his behind in trouble. He don't even play golf with Johnnie Cochran now. Same thing with Clinton. He all up in the black church now that he's in trouble. He didn't act like no brutha when he slammed Sista Souljah and Jesse Jackson some years back. Heck, Clinton be trying to play golf all the time too, just like the Juice."

"C'mon Bag, " I said. "Bill Clinton didn't kill anybody."

"O.J. said he didn't either," Bag retorted, "But there's a website that lists 'bout 52 people who knew Clinton that died. Kinda coincidental, huh?"

"Look, I'm really tired of all this Clinton stuff, Bag," I said. "I'm tired of all these so-called self-righteous people and so-called Christians trying to hold everyone else up to a higher standard than they can hold themselves."

"Hey man, I ain't out to crucify no Clinton neither," Bag said, "And I ain't gonna give him no soul shake either. I ain't no saint neither. I'm just trying to hold steady while the standards lower, just like everyone else."

It was Bag-Head Jheri, the Messanie Street philosopher, climbing out of a trash bin behind City Hall.

"Hey Bag-Head, how have you been? I haven't seen you in a while."

"Yeah, I know, Weston, now shut up and listen up. I got some rap for ya."

"Hey Bag, that isn't any way to be to a friend you haven't seen in awhile," I said, hurt.

"OK, my bad. Now shut up and listen. I'm telling ya, this sales-tax thing ain't gonna pass."

"And why not?" I asked. I knew he was referring to the sales-tax proposal on the August 8 ballot. If it passes, residents would have to pay a seven-eighths-cent sales tax that would ultimately generate about $8.2 million annually. About 75 percent of the money would go toward pay raises for the police and fire departments. The other 25 percent is supposed to go toward pay raises for other city workers.

"Well, for one thing, folks around here are getting pretty taxed out," Bag said. "They already twisted our arm to pass a property tax for the schools. We ain't had time to exhale and they shoving another one at us."

"Bag, don't you think these people deserve a raise? We can't expect to keep good help without paying good money for it," I tried to reason.

"Heck, I know a lot of folks that deserve raises here in this town that ain't gonna get none and don't care if the pohleese gets none either," Bag said.

"The money goes for the police AND the fire department AND the city workers," I reminded Bag.

"You don't think those cops ain't gonna be grabbin' most of the take?" Bag asked rhetorically. "And anyway, how they expect folks to pay another tax when their water bills are gonna go up, gas bills gonna go up and their light bills gonna go up? What would be the sense in working if all your paycheck gonna go towards taxes and utilities?"

"That's never going to happen, Bag," I said.

"Shoot, don't bet on it. You pass one tax and they want you to pass anothern' and anothern' and anothern'," Bag said. "Makes me wonder why some of them folks ever left England."

"C'mon, Bag. It isn't going to be that bad. What's seven-eighths of a cent?" I asked.

"It ain't the money, it's the principle. Why do I care if somebody asleep in a city truck gets a raise? If the cops want a raise then tell them to get it from one of them convenience stores. Seems like that's where they be doing all their patrolin'," Bag said.

"Folks can knock the police all they want, but the minute they have trouble, they don't hesitate to call 911," I said.

"Shoot, I've called taxi cabs that beat the cops to my house when I called em," Bag said. "I found out long ago that if you really want the cops, all you have to do is go sit in your car with two or three other black dudes. They'll come."

"C'mon, Bag you're joking now," I said.

"I'm as serious as a crack habit," Bag said. "I ain't putting out no money for these cops to be riding around styling and racial profiling in new cars."

"What are you worried about it all for anyway, Bag?" I asked. "You don't pay any taxes to speak of now."

"I know, but at the rate things are going, I might have to get a job," Bag said. "And with my luck, the only place that will be hiring will be Seaboard."

August 8, 2001

Editor's note: Alonzo Weston is on vacation. His friend and sometime mentor Bag-Head Jheri, the Messanie Street philosopher, will take over his "Street Smarts" column this week. Alonzo will return August 15.

First off, I ain't gonna tell y'all how please I am to be writing the column for Alonzo this week. Heck, if this newspaper was smart, I'd have my own weekly column anyway.

But I ain't one to look a gift horse in the mouth, so I thought that I could use this space to pull y'all's coattails to a few things that's been on my mind.

One thing I've been thinking about is these gov'ment checks that we all supposed to be getting. Now I know that I probably won't get any check and I can get with that. My income from collecting aluminum cans and scrap metal is tax-free.

So there ain't no shame in my game. But I can't help but wondering if them voters down in Florida will be getting any kind of a check? Now I ain't tryin' ta say the Republican Party done paid them off to get their boy elected, but I was just asking.

Somethin' else I been thinkin' about. What good is a measly $300 or $600 going to do anybody without a job? Shoot, that won't pay for a week of groceries in some folk's house. That's just going-to-the-gambling-boat money for some folks.

Why don't Bush put that money to use in some type a programs to train people to get better jobs or help them keep the job they have? Why don't he put the money into a program for better health care or something like that?

If he think that little bit of chump change gonna boost the economy, he is dumber than I thought. And I think he's dumber than a corncob anyways. I tell you something else I

178

think is stupid. I saw this CNN poll asking people if they think that kids today are spoiled. Now why would some big-time news outfit waste its time asking such a dumb question?

Now if you been buying your kid these designer jeans, a new PlayStation every time one come out and give them money without making them cut the grass for it or anything, who do you think they gonna be? Wally Cleaver or Bart Simpson?

I'll tell you how you can tell if your brat is spoiled. If something sits around too long it spoils, right? Well if all you see your kid doing is sitting around all the time talking on a cell phone, or playing video games, you know he's rotten spoiled. But don't worry, I got a cure for all that mess. Whip their behinds so they can't sit down. And when they are standing, give 'em a broom and shovel and shove 'em out tha' door into the real world. That's what I'd do. If they want money to go to the mall or somethin', make 'em earn it by do-ing something around the house.

It ain't no child abuse neither. Don't let nobody tell you that mess. A strappin' ain't no beatin.'

You see Alonzo don't write about nothin' like that. He'd rather write about his grandma and all that old stuff. He's too scared to break out the real Dily-O, so he'd rather let me do it. He knows I twang metal and settle and never back-pedal on any issue. I tell it like it is. Sometimes it's gotta be like that.

See y'all later.

The huge, clanking figure moved quickly toward me as I walked through downtown on a rainy Monday afternoon. It was just Bag-Head Jheri, the Messanie Street philosopher heading for the recycling center with two full bags of aluminum cans fastened to his belt.

He also carried a head full of thoughts that he couldn't wait to cash in with somebody. He thought I was buying.

"Weston, Ima tell ya' brother, these ain't no good times we living in today," Bag said.

"What do you mean, Bag? Things aren't that bad: the war is over, interest rates are down and we do live in America," I said.

"America is what I'm worried about," Bag shot back. "I tell ya' corporate greed is ruining this country. CEOs be voting themselves raises at the same time they cutting the wages of their workers. And that ain't all of it. Some of them be running off with folks' retirement money."

"Yeah, but some of those guys are paying for it, too. They are being brought up on charges and getting fined," I answered.

"Fined? What's a $2 million fine to someone making a billion dollars?" Bag asked rhetorically. "I think they oughta take everything they got by hook and crook and make them give it back to the people they stole it from."

"They're not going to do that," I said.

"Why not? They do it to the low-level criminals by making them pay restitution," Bag said. "They say we should bring dope dealers and hustlers down because they ruin communities. And don't get me wrong, they do. But these fancy rich guys are ruining the country. Tell me why they shouldn't be locked up for a long while."

"You're probably right, Bag," I said.

"Right here in St. Joe they talking about raising the water bill again," Bag said. "Now I ain't saying the water company is a bunch of criminals, but I wish I could give myself a raise anytime I wanted."

"It's still up to the Missouri Public Service Commission to approve the raise," I said.

"Trust me, this ain't no guessin' game. A bottle of Dasani bottled water will soon be costing less than our tap water," Bag said.

"I doubt that," I said.

"And this here thing about the Dixie Chicks and those actors protesting the Bush administration," Bag said, quickly changing the subject. "I thought we was over there fighting in Iraq to give those folks the same freedoms we be denying our people here. Is this still America?"

"Last time I checked it still was," I answered smartly.

"I don't know, Weston, it don't look much like America to me anymore," Bag said shaking his head. "It might look like it if you are rich and don't have to rely on state and federal funding to survive. You can't tell me with all these state and federal budget cuts to schools, social services and health, that we ain't gonna have some repercussions."

"I'm afraid you're right, Bag," I said while walking away.

"Having a job ain't even a guarantee of having the good life anymore," Bag said. "Pretty soon, cashing in cans to the recycling center might be the best job around. And I got seniority."

The hydraulic hissing of the tractor-trailer caught everyone's attention as it squeezed its way into the Hollywood Stadium 10 Theater parking lot last Thursday morning. Out of it jumped this huge clanking figure carrying a blue light saber.

Bag-head Jheri, the Messanie street philosopher, coming to see 'Star Wars?' I thought.

"Thanks for the ride, brutha man," Bag said to the semi driver as he slammed the cab door. He waddled over to where I was standing with some friends.

"Bag, I didn't know you were into 'Star Wars,'" I said as a greeting.

"A movie about a black dude taking over the universe and I'm gonna miss that?" Bag said.

"But Darth Vader isn't black," I corrected him. "He's a white guy wearing a black armored suit."

"There's plenty brothers walking 'round like that, if you dig my meaning," Bag said. "Besides, he sounds like James Earl Jones when he talks. That makes him black to me."

"Whatever, Bag," I said, giving up.

"What do you think going over to the dark side means, Weston?" Bag continued. "It ain't about no evil forces. It's about getting some soul in your stroll, you know?"

"You're not making any sense, Bag," I said.

"Eminem did it. Why can't this Skywalker kid?" Bag said. "Tell me something else, why are Billy Dee Williams and Samuel L. Jackson the only two other black folks in that whole universe? Where are the sistas?"

"C'mon, Bag, it's just a movie," I reasoned.

"Hey, I'm just sayin' I don't care what kinda force you got wit' you, you ain't gonna get rid of black women that easy," Bag said. "Tell me Pam Grier ain't gonna be up there getting eastside/westside with them storm troopers. When she pull that razor outta her afro uh-huh, hello."

"Bag, you're nuts," I said, holding back a chuckle.

"No man, I'm just keeping it real," Bag said. "Ain't no galaxy so far, far away that black folks can't piece together a hoopty and get there. Believe dat. And keep Jesse Jackson out too?"

"You aren't for real," I said, incredulously.

"I'm as real as a crack habit," Bag said. "Remember the album The Mothership Connection'? George Clinton and his funk group Parliament done been there way before Yoda."

"What?"

"That's right. That album came out before the first 'Star Wars' movie, so that makes us the original people in outer space too," Bag said seriously.

"Bag, look man, this is getting way too deep for me," I said while trying to get to the concession stand before the movie started. "It's all fantasy. 'Star Wars' is only a movie and 'The Mothership Connection' is only a record album."

"You always gotta read between the lines, brother," Bag said, completely ignoring me.

"I see you're real good at that."

The shiny black Lincoln Navigator had me jumping for cover as it pulled up on the curb. I thought it was an angry reader until I heard that laugh. That familiar growling, guttural-sounding "haw-huh-huh" of Bag-Head Jheri, the Messanie Street philosopher.

But driving an expensive SUV?

"Hey, Weston, haw-huh, check out my ride, baby," Bag said while grinning as he hopped out of the driver's seat of the luxury Lincoln. A barrage of aluminum cans tumbled out behind him.

"How on earth can you afford a ride like that, Bag, by selling aluminum cans?" I asked.

"Only in America, brutha' man," Bag said. "You gotta catch the American dream when it passes through, and it came rollin' through da' hood last night."

"What?" I asked, hoping for an explanation.

"This brutha came rollin' up in this here Nav'gator, asking if I take trade-ins, like I was some used car salesman or sumptin'," Bag explained. "Then he axed me to trade my Chuck Taylor Converses for his ride, said they'd be cheaper on gas."

"You mean he traded you his Lincoln Navigator for your old raggedy tennis shoes?" I asked incredulously.

"I ain't going to hell for lyin,'" Bag said.

"That just floors me. A guy trading in his SUV for a pair of tennis shoes," I said.

"You remember President Reagan's trickle-down economics? Well, it's finally done trickled down to us po' folks now," Bag said. "Those rich folks who done jumped up and bought those expensive houses and cars can't afford them now. They have to give all that stuff away. And you know when there's anybody givin' stuff away I'm the first to say hello. Ya' heard?"

"But Bag, how can you afford gas if some rich guy can't?" I asked.

"Brutha' when times are hard, that's when po' folks shine. We always live on nothin' so nothin' changed for us. Everything is everything." Bag said.

"Yeah, but you still gotta buy gas for that big Lincoln," I said.

"Baby, the convenience stores be looking like the post office now with all those wanted signs of people who done drove off without paying for gas," Bag said. "I ain't going to jail for no gas. I'll just drive this thing til' it runs out then I'll park it."

"What's the sense in having it then?" I asked.

"You gotta think like a po' man. I'll part it out and make me some serious money. How much you gimme for these spinner rims, brutha man?" Bag said.

"I don't need them," I answered. "But if you're so smart, Bag, how come you still riding around in a Navigator and picking up aluminum cans?"

"Hey man, like I said, times are tight," Bag said. "I ain't giving up my day job."

The enormous, hulking form clanking toward me couldn't be anyone else. No one but Bag-Head Jheri, the Messanie Street philosopher wears a plastic bag on his head and two trash bags full of aluminum cans strapped to his belt. No one.

"Hey, Bag, how are you?" I asked sincerely.

"Ah, Weston, everything is everything, and it's all good to the gracious, my brutha," Bag said while giving me an extended and convoluted soul handshake. "What's up with you, dog?" he asked back.

"Nothing really, Bag. Just going to work, taking care of business and getting ready for the Mardi Gras parade," I answered.

"Seen where folks had you and your roe dog, Sheehan, out there in traffic over that parade. Glad y'all didn't get run over," Bag said.

"Yeah, I just hope everything works out and everyone acts responsible this year," I said. "We even have new rules and regulations in place, and we're stressing again that this isn't a parade for kids. We want to help make sure things go well."

"Peep, this brutha, I ain't gonna lie to you. I ain't no prude. I did go to Mardi Gras last year cause I heard there was some naked girls down there," Bag said.

"Not that I wanted to, but I didn't see any nudity," I said. "Still, some folks said they got a lot of it on tape."

"On tape? Excuse me, but if you're offended by something, then why would you tape it unless you wanted to watch it over and over?" Bag asked. "Besides, if you really cared, why would you tape a supposedly half-naked underage girl instead of trying to get her to put on her clothes and go home or you'll call the cops?"

"I don't know, Bag, but I don't want to stir up that hornet's nest again," I said. "I just want the parade to go over without incident. Look, let's change the subject."

"OK, let's talk about reality shows. Man, those things need a reality check, know what I mean?" Bag asked.

"I don't watch them," I said.

"Take that one called Skating with Celebrities.' Last time Todd Bridges and Jillian Barberie were celebrities was way back when I got my first Jheri-curl. That was way back in 1980," Bag said. "If they going back to '80s stylin', at least they coulda brought back Gary Coleman and Mr. T."

"Maybe P-Diddy and Lindsay Lohan cost too much money," I reasoned.

"Look at that other show, Beauty and the Geek.' Who cares if some hot babe can assemble a computer? Those ain't the skills I'm looking for on my application. You hear me?" Bag said. "America Idol? Puh-leese. Why do I wanna hear somebody else's bad singing when I can listen to myself? Although I can warble a few tunes."

"Yeah, right. One last thing Bag, and I gotta go. What do you think about Oprah Winfrey's tongue-lashing of James Frey for lying in his memoir book, A Million Little Pieces?" I asked.

"Like whoa! When Oprah roars, everyone listens," Bag said. "But seriously, I don't think she woulda pulled down Toni Morrison or Alice Walker's file like that if they hadda done the same thing. If she did, you know that whole thing woulda went straight ghetto. Hello? Hair weaves woulda been flying everywhere."

"Yeah, maybe you're right, but hey, it's been good to see you, Bag. Don't stay away so long next time," I said.

"I think I'll slide to the left side and catch you on the flip side myself, bro' man," Bag said. "Later, dog."

ALL
THAT'S LEFT

Valentine's Day? Forget it! The good cards are for some-one else

If it's Valentine's Day, then I'm sorry for all the little boys out there today in some grade school classroom who, like me years ago, are getting all the Valentine's Day cards from the bottom of everybody's package.

You kids know what I'm talking about. You know what I'm talking about. You know when your momma buys you one of those cellophane packs of 30-some Valentine's Day cards to pass out to your classmates, the ones on the bottom are usually the worst ones or the misprints. You know very well that you save these for the most unpopular kids in your class.

If you're like I was, you're getting all of these cards that are full of typographical errors, or you hope they're typos, like, "You Won't Be My Valentine" and "I Don't Like You." If you're getting cards like these, wouldn't it be better if you just didn't get any Valentine's Day cards at all?

The teachers, bless their hearts, think they're doing the right thing by asking kids to bring cards for everybody. They think it would hurt a kid's feelings if he or she didn't receive any cards. They also think it teaches kids how to share.

But listen up teachers. Kids know about sharing. By the fifth grade, most of them have brought a cold or the flu and shared it with the rest of the class several times. The kids that were left out of that sharing, I'm sure didn't mind.

To be honest, I too picked out the best Valentine's Day cards to give to all the girls I liked. The girls I didn't like, at least I was polite to them. I just sent them to the bland and simple cards that said things like "Have A Happy Valentine's Day" or "Be Nice."

I never sent any good ones to any of the guys in my class, either. The lovely, heartfelt sentiments like "Be My Valentine" or "Lot's of Kisses on Valentine's Day," would become fighting words in that context.

There is always one girl in everybody's class who gets the best cards from all the guys and some of the girls. That girl in our third grade class at Horace Mann School was named Marilyn. I remember spending half the night before Valentine's Day trying to find the card that expressed just exactly how I felt about her. Goofy and Donald Duck just couldn't do it.

"I Love You" and "Kiss Me," sounded too obvious. "Be My Valentine" sounded too unimaginative. It sounded like something a caveman would scrawl on a wall after he dragged some girl into his cave.

No, the card I wanted for dear Marilyn had to have just the right mix of subtlety, intrigue, mystery, and romance. I had to figure out a way to let her know just how passionate and worldly I really was, all in five words or less and with a cartoon character on the cover of a card.

I usually settled on something from "Lady and the Tramp" or from Popeye and Olive Oyl.

I never found out to whom Marilyn sent all of her good cards. I don't think I ever got one. The ones I got from her always sounded vague like "I'm Sure" ("I'm Sure" what? You're an idiot?), or they were one of the misprints.

Some young boy out there in class somewhere today is sitting there with his sweaty hands folded on his desk and dreading the hour when the teacher passes out the Valentine's cards. He has no reason to believe that this will be the year he gets all the good cards. He hasn't yet, and it's already late in the fifth or sixth grade. So, here's to all of you, "Have a Happy Valentine's Day."

Halloween was one night you could break Mom's strictest rules

When I was a kid, Halloween was the date the lease ran out on the summer breeze and the winter wind started moving in.

It was a time when only the most stubborn of leaves still clung to the trees. It was the true end of summer.

It was just Halloween, and it bore no resemblance to the evil, Satanic thing that some folks believe it is today.

It was also the one night of the year when I was allowed to break two of mom's strictest rules. I didn't have to be home before dark. And I could beg food from the neighbors.

I liked it too because it was the one time I didn't have to dress like the other kids. I could be different in a good way for once. I could dress as goofy and act as weird as I wanted and still fit in with the crowd.

Just one Halloween night made up for all the days I got sent home from school for not following the school dress code.

I could dress up as anything that was on the Halloween costume rack at Katz Drug Store. That was because my mother and grandmother worked there and could afford to buy me a store-bought costume with their employee discount.

When money was tight, many of us kids just made our costumes out of old clothes. It was easy because kids clothes had three lives then. When you got new school clothes, your old school clothes became your play clothes. Your old play clothes became either household rags or the only garments you were allowed to shred with scissors and make into Halloween costumes without getting into trouble.

If you made your own costume this way, all you had to spend money on was black face paint, which was cheap.

Sure, we were blacks in black-face. But it was before the civil rights movement, so no one really cared if your disguise made you look like vagrant Al Jolson. It was also before people started putting poison on candy or razor blades in apples. Or, maybe it was before some people started talking about other people doing these things, and it became urban legend.

The only Halloween handouts we hated getting were pennies and unsolicited advice from stingy old men in the neighborhood.

The pennies we could find on the street. As for the advice and the lectures, we already got more than we could ever want from our parents and other adults every day.

All we wanted was enough candy, apples, and oranges to fill a brown paper grocery bag to the top. It had to be an amount that looked impressive to the other kids when you spilled it all out on the kitchen table at the end of the night. Not counting the portion you knew you would inevitably lose after getting caught in school with it by your teacher, you at least hoped you'd get enough candy to last you a month.

That's all I ever knew of all I ever wanted to know about Halloween as a kid. I knew nothing about Satan worship or any ancient Celtic festival of the dead. I hope the kids who knock on my door tonight don't know anything about such things either. I sure won't tell them.

It's hard to be humble when you're a 'big feeler'

My grandmother used to despise "big feelers."

She described "big feelers" as people who thought they were better than everyone else. They are the people who demand attention, not by their charisma or some impressionable aura, but by their grating pomposity and "look at me" attitude.

She never actually said it, but she conveyed the feeling that the world would be a better place if everyone were more humble.

For years, I never believed that was actually true. Like many people, I mistook being humble for being weak and lacking self-confidence. I believed that to succeed you had to have a substantial amount of cockiness and arrogance and self-promotion. You simply had to prove you were better than everyone else.

In a sense, some of that's true. Because so much of the world is based on competition, it seems you have to have an edge to even survive sometimes.

But being a "big feeler" is a different thing. It's about believing no one else is worth anything except you. It's about looking down on people who are different or have less than you.

Hitler was a "big feeler." Farrakhan is a "big feeler."

Mark Fuhrman and David Duke are "big feelers."

Not many people would care to associate with this motley crew, but anytime you judge someone or stereotype someone, I believe you tread the same ground.

I always used to be shy and could never take a compliment, and for a long time, I mistook that for being humble.

But my wife always says that when she first met me, I had this cocky, strutting, arrogant air about me that gave me away.

194

I used to get mad when, after I started writing for this paper, people would say that they didn't think I wrote this stuff. Some were joking, some were not.

I was angry because they felt I had no talent, when I knew that many of these people didn't know me at all. Was it my own subliminal cockiness coming to the surface again that demanded the respect? If I were truly humble, it wouldn't have mattered what they thought.

The more I thought about it, the more I realized there is a fine line between arrogance, self-confidence, and humility. Perhaps, I have been so wrapped up in wanting respect that I had forgotten that my writing is a God-given talent.

My being able to write comes from family, friends, and people I've met throughout my life. I know this to be true, because if I lived in a void or a vacuum with no interpersonal interaction, I wouldn't have anything to write about.

I am merely the vehicle used to convey God's gift and these experiences.

Once I figured this out—that I needed other people to write—it was easy to be humble. We need the grace of God and the love of other people in this life anyway, if we are going to survive.

Really, the only thing we're here for is to help one another and to be humble doing it. As usual, my grandmother was right.

Count it as a blessing if you have somewhere you can float

It took me a while to learn how to float. I just couldn't bring myself to trust something as uncaring as water.

Water didn't care if I could swim. It didn't care if I drowned.

But water is bound by its own laws. It has to support me when I don't support myself. It has to support me when I let go. Even a dead man knows how to float.

Once I learned to trust water enough to float inside it, I realized there were other places I had been floating in all along.

These were places where I could let my defenses down.

I could allow myself to be buoyed by my surroundings. There are people and places I know that support me and lift me up.

On holidays I float inside my family. I let my guard down and allow their spirits to carry me through the day. Like floating is becoming one with the water, I am part of them. I will hold a sparkler for my baby granddaughter today. I want her to trust that I won't let it burn her. I want her to trust and to know that I, like water, will always be there to support her.

Water is bound by its laws of buoyancy. My laws of love bound

A few years ago I lost an old friend who never learned to float. She never learned to trust that anyone would support her whenever she let go of her defenses.

In the darkest hours of one Independence Day morning, she took her life. She died all alone, afraid to let go and allow herself to float in the love and trust of someone else. It hurts when I think that she didn't even trust me enough.

But floating is probably the first and hardest lesson in learning how to swim. Trust is probably the first and hardest lesson in learning how to live.

We go under a few times and become afraid of the water—or someone else.

I know I am blessed whenever I can float inside my wife, my children, my mother, my father, my brothers, sisters, aunts, uncles, cousins and good friends. And they can float inside me. It is with their support I'm able to be all I can be. I support them all the same. I know I am blessed when I can float inside my church. I can let go and feel the love and support of all those around me. And I become part of that support too. Like water, we are bound by law to support and bring back to the top the people who fall.

Count it as a blessing if you have somewhere you can float. Count it as a blessing if you can find at least one person who loves and supports you regardless of who you are or what you've done.

Too many times the laws that bind family and friends are not as strong as the principles that bind water. Something as uncaring and as impartial as water will always support us while those who are supposed to care about us will sometimes let us sink.

As you picnic and shoot off fireworks today, float inside the love of your family and friends. If not, find someone who will let you float today, who will let you let go and be yourself today. Let someone float inside you.

My condolences go out to the family of George Sherman. Mr. Sherman, who died Monday, was an old newspaperman and a man whom I admired and respected. Just to listen to the stories he told and the way he told them was always a treat. He always had just the right mix of cockiness and charm. I'll surely miss him.

Age brings wisdom of sorts during stroll on carnival midway

The maturity of years and television has jaded my gullibility at carnivals. After all, being somewhat easily influenced or credulous is what allows you to enjoy yourself at the carnivals.

You have to actually believe you can win that stuffed animal with one throw of the softball or one swing of the hammer. You have to believe wholeheartedly that the games are not rigged in one way or another. It helps, too, if you're the type that routinely watches WWF wrestling. Then it all comes easy.

But I was amazed at my control as I walked through the midway of Evans Shows' carnival with my wife last weekend.

It seemed almost biblical, as we looked neither left nor right but kept on the straight-and-narrow path, while we ignored the many guys and gals who leered from gaudy, noisy booths and cooed temptations at us.

And we would have fallen if a five-foot, purple stuffed gorilla or a framed Metallica photo were one of our weaknesses.

I've seen enough "Banned from TV" and news shows to never trust carnival rides again. No matter if one out of a million rides malfunctions once in a millennium, I still don't trust them.

Besides, the last time I rode a carnival ride, which was something perfectly named "The Scrambler," I had gastric problems for a week. It wasn't my brain, but my stomach, that felt more like the scrambled egg frying in the pan on that "This is your brain on drugs..." commercial.

But there was a time when I never got indigestion from a carnival ride. And there was a time when I felt I could win any carnival game put before me. It was in the days when they used to let kids out early for the Apple Blossom Parade.

In those days, the carnival accompanied the parade.

They went together like cotton candy and pinwheels. And it was more of a time rather than an event. Together they gave a tangible quality to our anticipation for summer and our sigh of relief at winter's demise.

Today, the carnival often comes in the night and sets up in a desolate part of town, like the evil circus in the Ray Bradbury novel "Something Wicked This Way Comes," and completely separate from the parade.

I used to spend whatever money I had in my pockets at the carnival and not feel ashamed about it. I would throw 50 softballs to knock three wooden monkeys off a shelf to try and win a straw hat or water gun. I know I could have gotten both items much cheaper at Kresge's department store, but it meant more to win them.

I once spent $80 trying to pick the duck with the lucky number out of a metal stream that was rigged up in a carnival booth. Sure, I never found the duck, but the fun of trying was worth every bit of the money. And I had no doubt that I wouldn't find it and no suspicion that the game was fixed.

No one ever got killed on a carnival ride then either. If they did, we never heard about it. We rode everything without fear.

I left the carnival that night a week ago without riding or buying anything, or playing any games. I'm too wise for all that silliness now. I'd long since learned that the rides and the sugary, carnival food could kill you.

But I saw some kids and adults laughing and having a good time. They were playing the games and riding everything. I admit, I envied their ignorance.

Most men will eventually do battle with Dorian Gray

I've heard it said for many years: "He's going through a mid-life crisis." And it would always come from a woman, never another man, about some man in his 40s or 50s who buys a red sports car, or dyes his hair or hangs out with people who are young enough to be his children.

When I was a kid, I'd see women shake their heads and go, "um, um, um" as some older guy would be driving down the street in a sports car with some young girl on his side or wearing teenager clothes and a toupee. The men would always chuckle to themselves and wink at each other until the women would give them a glaring stare. Then the men would slink off into the garage, bar, pool hall or somewhere else where they had the freedom to discuss the situation candidly.

I overheard one of these discussions years ago and learned that it isn't such a psychological thing but an actual battle with Dorian Gray that every man in mid-life must fight.

Dorian Gray is a protagonist in the 1890 book by Oscar Wilde entitled, The Picture of Dorian Gray.' In the book and the movie, Dorian Gray has this picture that ages while he stays forever young. The picture he keeps hidden in a closet spares his vanity by bearing the ravages of time and the excesses of his life. It shows all the wrinkles, the gray hair and the deep facial lines earned by Gray but not owned up to.

When every man fights against the spirit of Dorian Gray, he fights for the right to age gracefully. The loser gets the hair dye. I had my first encounter with Dorian Gray some years ago when I started getting my first gray hairs. It was in my bathroom late one night when he appeared in my mirror and tried to get me to use a bottle of Grecian formula. Through the looking glass I went, wrestling to the ground with Gray to keep him from pouring the stuff on my head. I was spared then by my wife, who heard the commotion and came running into the bathroom, jerked the stuff out of my hand and flushed it. Another time I wasn't so lucky. He got me down and poured the stuff on me one night when I was half asleep and turned what then had become a gray stripe into a blonde one. He laughed; so did everyone else.

I managed to avoid him for a while after that—that is, until a few weeks ago. He caught me alone in the bathroom again late one night, yanked me through the mirror, gagged me so I couldn't scream and poured hair dye on my head. My wife couldn't save me that time.

Now I must walk through life with the battle scar of hair that is too black. The symbol for everyone to see that I lost the fight with Dorian Gray. "What did you do to your hair, Alonzo?" asked the smirking woman. I didn't answer her. This old gray-haired man in his 80s, who was standing nearby, overheard her. He put his hand on my shoulder and he led me away.

He whispered in my ear: "Someday you'll win, son. Someday you'll win the battle against Dorian Gray."

Too old to cruise, too young for Oats - call this the mid-40s

I'm old and I'm out of shape. There, I've conceded it finally.

No, I'm not "over-the-hill" or "senior-citizen-discount old." But I'm old enough that words I once used like "Whopper," "chocolate malt" and "fried chicken" have been replaced in my culinary lexicon by terms such as "cholesterol," "low fat," "arteries" and "blood pressure."

I'm just old enough to look in the hair-dye section at the drug store with intent. If I were senior-citizen old, I wouldn't worry about it. But I'm just at that age where I don't feel old mentally, but physically. My mind is beginning to make promises my body can't fulfill.

My mind tells me I can hang with the 20-somethings on the basketball court across from my house. But last summer, when we were choosing sides, my son picked me last. He said he didn't pick me because he wanted to compete against me, but no one else did either. I knew. My son beats me in arm wrestling now, too. I was never any good at it anyway.

I decided a few months ago to go back to the gym. I wanted to recapture that V-shaped torso I once had as a young man who religiously lifted weights. I looked good in my clothes then. I tucked everything in to show off my flat stomach and broad chest. I'm shaped like a "B" now and have an uncontrollable urge to wear all my shirttails out. The tank tops I used to wear look like maternity tops.

My workout regimen now consists of a month in the gym with a month at the doctor's office. I do my reps with a dumbbell in one hand and a pain pill in the other. I no longer buy cologne because the Ben-gay smell overpowers everything anyway.

My wife has been buying my clothes for some time now.

She tries to make me feel better by saying, "This is how all the rappers and grunge artists and young people dress. They all wear their clothes now extra large."

Yeah, but they fit me.

I know I'm old because I take more antacids and still belch and do the gas thing now. When you're young, such events either caused embarrassment or laughter. When you're old, people don't even look at you or say a word, almost as if you didn't do anything. They just leave the room—quickly. And you sometimes may not realize you did anything either. That sort of stuff gets trickier in old age.

I know I'm old now too, because I buy underwear now not for its sexiness, but for its support. I buy cars for comfort and not for looks. My kids' friends call me "Mr." and look at me like I used to look at old people who still think they're young—with a smirk.

Learning to walk often requires an entirely new outlook on life

I started walking. Now when you hear that, you can pretty much figure it can only come from one of two people: a toddler that's just learning how to walk, or a middle-aged, overweight, cholesterol-laden guy whose doctor told him to exercise.

But I fall somewhere in the middle. Sure, I am overweight and almost middle age (or past it, depending on which insurance chart you go by), but I am learning how to walk again. I can stroll along with the best of them when it comes to walking in a grocery store or at the mall. I don't even need a cane or one of those aluminum things that look like a portable guard- rail.

I have to learn to walk aerobically or at least good enough not to look like a fool on Ashland Avenue.

You have to be cool to walk on Ashland Avenue because everybody will see you. You can't wear just any old pair of sweats and a T-shirt and walk like some hick that's lost in a big city. You either have to have a jogging suit or name brand shoes or shirt and you have to walk like you've been there before. Don't ooh and ahh at all the neat houses you walk past and don't wave at all the cars driving by. That's what rookies do. You want to look like a pro, like you've seen it all before.

And you have to walk fast enough to get some aerobic benefit. You can't just stroll down Ashland like you're walking to the movies. And you can't be seen hugging any trees or any other vertical thing trying to catch your breath.

That's why I just walk in my neighborhood. People there know me and they know that I'm out of shape. They've seen me leaning on their trees and stooped over several times in the general area, trying to get my second wind. They also know that nothing I ever wear matches, either. I'll wear Oakland Raiders shorts, a Tennessee Volunteers T-shirt and a Utah Jazz cap and no one in my neighborhood will even look twice. But I'll bet they talk about me all the same.

"That's that Alonzo Weston," they probably say. "I've heard his wife has to dress him for work" Or, "If he'd do some yard work once in awhile, he wouldn't be so out of shape and passed out in my flowerbed."

Just the fact that I'm walking and not running says a lot. Walking on the street, whether it's Ashland Avenue or the parkway, means you're just one step away from walking in the mall.

You're not far from wearing those clean, white Rockports that are popular with the uh… mature walker. And you're not far from wearing the same warm-up suit as your wife. Only if you stole something, do you run in the mall.

I do notice that walkers and runners alike are usually more courteous than drivers. On foot, no one ever cuts you off or flips someone the bird or runs red lights. If you don't have a few tons of metal around you, it's apparent you'll want to yield the right of way to someone who does.

Another thing about walking are the small animals. Dogs, cats, squirrels and the like are no problem when you're in a car. Most of us hardly even notice when we run over a squirrel or a small dog until we go to the car wash. You can even tease dogs when you're in a car. When you walk, it's another story. All animals can outrun you, run longer than you and catch you, so you have to be nice to all of them when you walk

Really, walking isn't so bad. If you're like me, crawling isn't too bad either. And my mother always says you've got to crawl before you walk.

Deciding whether to play or stay home can be a tough decision

We lose a lot of things as we get older. One of those things is the sense of knowing when it is time to quit.

Many of us, when we get past our prime, still think we can do some of the same things we used to do as teenagers. We think we can still fit into the same clothes—and we can, we just don't do up the belt.

Some of us think we can still play the same games that young people play. There are plenty of old guys still trying to compete with the young guys in the single bars or on the basketball court and hoping that no one notices them gasping for air.

Back in the day, all of us kids used to hate it when some grown-ups would try to join our pickup basketball games.

Out of respect or fear or both we didn't dare say no, we let them play. Out of that same respect or fear, we slowed the game down for them. We let them make uncontested lay-ups and shots. We fed them the ball endlessly. We groaned but we listened as they told us how the game was really supposed to be played, no dunking, no behind-the-back dribbles or fade-away jumpers.

If the old-timer happened to be on your team, you fed him the ball until he got tired, which didn't take long, or until his wife or some other adult told him to leave us alone.

To be fair, there were some of these older guys who joined our kid games who were still good ball players. We didn't have to give them any free shots or lay-ups. We would need their condescension. They played us hard, and they wanted us to play them hard too. They still had game.

I think about this as I think about Michael Jordan today.

According to a number of reports, the former NBA great is speculating a comeback after being retired for almost three years.

If he does decide to come back and play basketball again, I wonder in which group he would fall.

Would he provoke the same playground pathos among the young members of the league that we as kids had for the old guys who showed up to play on our court?

Or would he take yet another class of ball players to school on the basketball court? Would he amaze us and dazzle us like never before?

At 38 years old, Jordan would be around the same age as Karl Malone and John Stockton of the Utah Jazz. Both of them are still good, but no longer great, players. Both of them have never stopped playing, they're still in basketball shape. That is the difference.

I personally wish Michael Jordan would stay retired.

What does he have to prove? He's already considered the greatest. The league is looking for the next Michael Jordan, not the old one.

Some of the sorriest sights I have seen have been in the world of sports. Most of them were when some guy stayed too long or tried to make a comeback way past his prime.

It was really sad to see Muhammad Ali get beat on by a younger Larry Holmes. It was embarrassing to see James "Quick" Tillis become James "Slow" Tillis while impersonating a side of aged beef for Rob Calloway to punch last Friday night.

I even thought it was sad to see Joe Montana in a Chiefs uniform, as Kansas City has long been the place where old quarterbacks go to die.

I knew it was time to quit and start playing with guys my own age a few years back. I tried to join my son and a couple of his friends in a pickup basketball game across the street from my house. The only thing that made me feel young again was that I was picked last. That hadn't changed since childhood.

But I did well after the game started. I could drive to the basket and shoot at will. No one dared get in my way. They fed me the ball and just stood back and watched.

It was too easy. That's why I just played one game and went home.

Stay home, Michael.

A 60-year-old man did what?

As of Tuesday, I'm a 60-year-old man.

When you read the words "60-year-old man" somewhere, it's usually followed by something the person did that was extraordinarily athletic for his age or something incredibly senior-moment stupid.

A 60-year-old man either swims the English Channel or forgets the gas and brake pedal configuration and drives into a convenience store window. Other than that, he fades into senior citizen invisibility. TV commercials don't target him. There're no store or magazine ads designed for him.

Friends wished me happy birthday on Facebook for more than a week leading up to my birthday. Although I truly appreciated their birthday wishes, it felt like a shove over the threshold into old-manhood. I was leaving the colorful Oz of my youth and heading into a world of grayness, flatulence and wrinkles.

All year long, I tried holding on to my 50s. I gladly signed my age with a five still in front of it on everything I could. I felt the six bearing down on me.

Fifty-nine is a lot like being 29 years old in some ways. Turning 30 is the first sign you pass heading out of your youth. After that, the 40s, 50s and 60s are like mile markers on a road that's all downhill. A road that ends with a dead end.

When I turned 50, it seemed bad at first. Applications for AARP memberships, toilet lifts, shower chairs, handrails, medical alert devices and ads for other assistance devices began showing up in my mailbox.

Throwing all that junk mail in the trash felt like a bold act of defiance. I refused to let the reminders of my creeping old age clutter up my life.

But somewhere in the years, I got comfortable with 50. I remembered Clint Eastwood was still fist fighting in movies after he turned 50. Denzel Washington and Jack Nicholson were still considered hip and cool in their 50s. That meant it was OK.

I've always gauged my age by sports and action hero movies anyway. When I turned 30, it was OK because there were guys still playing pro football at that age.

Jerry Rice, Brett Favre and Warren Moon still played football in their 40s. Nolan Ryan was still throwing heat at 42 years old. George Foreman reclaimed his heavyweight title at 45 years old. At 60, now I look for other 60-year-olds who are still in sports or leading men in movies.

The only people in the NFL close to 60 are the kickers. Gary Player made the cut at the Masters one year at the age of 63. And 60-year-old men can still play pool and poker.

Sylvester Stallone, Robert DeNiro and Liam Neeson are still kicking behind in action movies. Actually, 63-year-old Liam Neeson didn't really start playing tough guys until he began to approach 60. Before that, he usually played solemn, serious characters in movies like "Schindler's List."

Now he's drop-kicking gangs of Middle Eastern terrorists. And here I am just the cranky old man trying to keep bullies off the playground near my house.

I recently bought a book at a garage sale entitled "60 Things To Do When You Turn 60." Surprisingly, it was 374 pages long.

One chapter said I could live another 40 years if I had good genes, a healthy dose of optimism, exercise and don't smoke. (The book smells as if it once belonged to a smoker. The previous owner either died or gave up on the book due to poor health.) The book also advised that I drink eight glasses of water every day, walk my dog, eat chocolate and, for whatever reason, go to Alaska.

There's one chapter entitled "Take off Your Clothes." It said I can wear purple or go naked now. Uhhhhh, no. If you see me somewhere naked in public, you know I've escaped from a nursing home somewhere and had long since forgotten or given a damn what 60 even was.

My smart phone makes me cool now

I got a smart phone. Finally.

For some of you, that's like hearing I've finally learned how to eat at the table. That's how elementary having a smart phone is for some people. Smart phones have been around long enough now that they even have them for toddlers.

For $12 you can buy a toddler smart phone with colorful buttons that make just as many offensive sounds as the real thing. You've got to start them young if you want them to be suitably distracted by their teenage years.

Toddler smart phones have been out for a while now. So that means some 6-month-old baby, probably lots of them, has owned one way before I did. That puts me behind the learning curve of a kid who's not even a year old.

But that's what happens when you get to a certain age. Young kids begin to do things better than you and much faster than you do. My granddaughter knows her way around a computer much better than I do.

When I'm on the computer, it's like she sees me as an old person driving below the speed limit and she's creeping impatiently behind me.

"Here Papa, let me do it for you," she says as she politely moves my hand off the keys. Yeah, get out of the way, old man.

But I got a smart phone because my wife felt I needed one. So one Saturday afternoon she took my hand like she would a toddler and walked me to the phone store. I actually looked around for a jar of suckers on the counter when I first walked in. Of course, there were none, just lots of phone choices and different plans to pay for them.

I had just bought a new flip phone about a year ago and it worked fine. But people laughed as if I rode in on a donkey whenever I flipped it open. I actually took pride in my old flip phone. I defiantly pushed back against the rush of technology. I'm old school, baby, and proud of it.

Yet there I was at the counter speaking with a young lady who spoke in a language I didn't understand.

"Do you want Android or iPhone?" "What about OS compatibility?" "How many apps will you load?" "GPS navigation?"

I felt like a foreigner in my own land. I looked to my wife for a translation.

"He doesn't need anything too fancy. This is his first smart phone," my wife said. The saleswoman gave me a look as if I had just got out of prison or crawled out of a cave after 20 years.

What free, working, walking-around man doesn't have a smart phone? the look said.

After three hours explaining the workings of the phone, I finally bought one, an Android phone (Still don't know what that means. A robot made to resemble a human?) and headed out the door.

"Well, now you have to buy a cover and a screen protector," my wife said.

"What did I buy? A TV?" I answered. "I thought this was it."

So after we went back to buy those things, I was finally a proud smart phone user. Now I can sit at restaurant table and check my phone constantly like all the hip people. I can now learn to master the skill of driving while texting.

Need Willie McCovey's lifetime batting average? Ask me. I'll Google it on my phone! I even have apps and an app killer too!

And now everywhere I go, I feel compelled to let people know where I'm at via my smart phone.

"I'm eating at Gates BBQ." "I'm at the Mustangs game." This is stuff only my burglar wants to know.

But I've finally moved into the 21st century, by golly, and, man, is it strange.

Bopp Files
August 30, 1995

I have a whole computer file of unfinished stories, thoughts and column ideas that I call the "Bopp File." "Bopp" is my nickname. These are story ideas that I've either got from people or weird stuff I think about when lying under my bed in a fetal position.

The "Bopp File" is growing so huge it's threatening to take over my other files like some huge fungus. So I figured it would be a wise practice to clean it out from time to time.

Here are just a few of the throwaway musings from the "Bopp File":

Why are we never satisfied with the weather? When it's hot outside we want it so cold inside our homes we have to wear earmuffs and thermal underwear. When it is cold outside we want it hot enough inside to bake a turkey.

My son always thought it had to do with control. You can't control anything else in your life, but at least you can control the thermostat.

I have a friend who listened to country music for most of his life. He immediately sobered up when he stopped listening.

He also had this to say: "Outside of bartenders and psychiatrists, most people don't care to listen to other people moan about their problems. But these same people will plop down $15 for a recording of someone wailing and complaining and play it over and over. They'll even buy $40 tickets to go see them do it in person."

Waiters and waitresses survive on tips. Salespeople rely on sales commissions. A wife of a friend of mine, who is a saleswoman, complained that many of her friends brag to her about buying huge, costly items in her store but they let someone else sell it to them. If they were real friends they'd wait until they could buy it from her so she could get the commission.

I hear this too much: "Ain't it a shame the way kids nowadays just have to have expensive, name-brand clothing?" It's a shame there's so many violent movies and rap music out there destroying our kid's minds."

I say: "Why do these complaining parents buy their kids these expensive clothes if they can't afford it or don't want their kids to wear them? Kids don't run the companies that distribute violent rap music or make violent movies—adults do.

I see where some judges, as part of probation restrictions for some black offenders, forbid them from being on Messanie Street. I've never seen a white person banned from the Belt Highway. Maybe I missed it.

I can't hear it, but I know somewhere a tree is falling in a forest. I can't see it, but I know somewhere in St. Joseph someone is getting a parking ticket.

My mom, like everyone else who works at the East Hills Shopping Center, has two jobs but only gets paid for one. While doing their jobs at the mall for which they are paid, she and other employees also have to watch the children of parents who mistake the mall for a day-care center.

My mom said she doesn't change diapers.

July 23, 1997

You wouldn't believe how dusty it is in here. I can't remember the last time I went to my computer attic and cleaned out my "Bopp File."

The "Bopp File" is a computer file where I store all my unfinished column ideas, news stories and just plain weird stuff I come across. I toss all sorts of things into it from time to time and forget about it until this computer icon—it looks mysteriously like my wife—pops up on the screen and demands that I clean out my computer attic.

Well there aren't any good ball games on television, and my daughter's already cut the grass, so I might as well put on some gloves and old work clothes and get busy:

What's with all these brand new houses sitting vacant in Midtown for well over a year? Who were they built for? Why hasn't anyone moved into them yet?

I heard the Housing Authority and the city of St. Joseph that built the houses can't decide on criteria for who should be eligible to move in. If they don't decide soon, the hobos, winos, roaches and rats will decide for them.

You'd be advised to take a canteen and a box of Wet Wipes if you plan to visit one of our All-America city parks. They're waterless. Somebody came up with the bright idea to turn off all the water in the park bathrooms to discourage vandals. Well it didn't work. I saw this mad mama with a messy kid on her hip rip the faucets out of the wall up in Krug Park the other day.

I can't wait until I get my wings so I can walk on water like some Christians are doing nowadays. Wouldn't it be nice to be perfect so you could condemn everyone who isn't? Then again, even Jesus Christ didn't do that.

I was watching Kung Fu the other night and found myself thinking it would have been neat to have been raised by an old Chinese master who talked in parables and carried a big staff.

Then I realized my grandmother, who reared me, also talked in parables and carried a big stick.

I never thought I'd say this, but this year I'm looking forward to Trails West!, that annual, opulent, cowboy extravaganza. The promoters really do try to offer something for everyone. Some of us like jazz, some of us like bluegrass and country and some of us like funk. So what did the Trails West! people do? They brought in the popular bluegrass-jazz-funk band, Bela Fleck and the Flecktones. These guys are great. Hats off to the Trails West! crew.

October 24, 2001

I went to clean out the Bopp File the other day, and all of this stuff came tumbling out:

A reader called the other day and expressed concern about cocaine users in these anthrax-threatening times.

The reader wanted me to write a public service announcement cautioning cocaine users to think twice before sniffing any white powder up their noses.

Instead of a quick high, she feared they could be getting a speedy anthrax death.

Somehow it seemed redundant to me. Was there ever a time when a cocaine user could trust the dust? It has always killed people.

Why in the world would anybody name a school lunch item "John Marzetti?" Asking your kids what they had for lunch and having them answer, "We ate John Marzetti," just doesn't sound right to me. It sounds like cannibalism.

To find out where the name came from, I asked my colleague and good friend, News-Press columnist and graphic artist Jim Finlay, whom I consider somewhat of an expert on these type of questions. Jim is, next to John Schellhorn down at Wire Rope, probably the funniest man in St. Joseph.

He found a site on the Internet that said the "John Marzetti" dish was named after the owner of the Marzetti Restaurant in Columbus, Ohio. He created the simple-but-popular casserole dish, which consists of meat, pasta and tomato sauce, in the early 1920s.

Heck, I used to make sandwiches out of peanut butter and Karo syrup when I was a kid. I wonder if I can call them "Alonzo Westons?"

Also in Ohio, it was reported in the Cleveland Plain Dealer that a Cleveland City Council member is trying to get legislation passed that would fine youths for wearing pants that sag too low. The law, if passed, would hit offenders with a $25 fine for wearing their pants in the low-slung style popularized by rappers and, inadvertently, overweight refrigerator repairmen.

I'd like to see a similar law in St. Joseph passed against tight jeans, bright-colored western shirts and big belt buckles.

Make no mistake, South Side activist Juanita Crockett is a proud grandmother. Folks are probably still talking about the pictures of her granddaughter she was showing off at the Pony Express Historical Association's annual hot dog roast two Sundays ago.

The pictures were in the Budweiser 2001 Women of the University of Kansas calendar. Her granddaughter, Meagan Crockett, a 20-year-old business major and dark-haired beauty, is Miss April.

"It's not easy to raise one like that," Mrs. Crockett beamed. "She's a good-looking one, and she's an A student too. It makes me feel pretty proud."

It's time again to clean out the Bopp file. You know, that computer file where I keep my unfinished columns, story ideas, foolish thoughts and just plain weird stuff.

Well, it's time to clean it out again. Here's some stuff I'm throwing out:

First, I'd like to thank God for the good weather and everyone else for making this year's Coleman Hawkins Jazz Festival a success. Everyone from the crowd, the performers, the vendors and members of the Coleman Hawkins Jazz Society worked together beautifully. A special thanks goes to Erich Uhlhorn who came in on a moment's notice to do our sound. Heck, he even brought some of his own equipment.

Many were disappointed with one of our acts showing up late. Gerald Dunn and the Jazz Disciples showed up well over an hour late Saturday evening. But the Wild Women of Kansas City showed up early and gave us a longer and greatly entertaining show.

But Gerald Dunn is a class act. He apologized profusely and said he would hold a fund-raiser for our Coleman Hawkins Jazz Society at the Blue Room in Kansas City.

Speaking of Kansas City, why on earth would they hold their first 18th and Vine Rhythm and Ribs festival on the same weekend we hold our jazz festival?

The Coleman Hawkins Jazz Fest was born before Rhythm and Ribs. And out of respect for our organization and for jazz itself, it would have been nice if we could have got together and worked something out.

But at least Rhythm and Ribs was held some 50 miles away. The Rendezvous Restaurant had a band playing right across the street during our festival Friday night.

I guess the easy money they make off the crowd from our Coleman Hawkins Mardi Gras parade isn't enough.

Went to Judy's D&G one evening last week and saw a familiar sight behind the bar. Pete Minor is back.

Welcome back, Pete, we missed you. The D&G truly wasn't the same without you, man.

Saw Jermaine Jackson on the news the other day. He was telling folks how wrong they were about his brother Michael Jackson. And one of the things he said was that Mike never slept with children.

Now everyone's heard Michael admit several times that he did sleep with children. He said it was purely innocent.

But I knew right off when I saw Jermaine still wearing that outdated Jheri-Curl hairstyle that he was way behind the curve on some things.

I'm old enough to remember the days when it was an unwritten rule among blacks that you speak when you saw a member of your own race. Blacks who didn't were considered rude or uppity.

Now I see quite a few other blacks, not all young ones, play like "The Exorcist" when they see another member of their own race. I've seen them spin their heads all the way around so they won't have to speak.

Other blacks, not just around here but in other parts of the country, have noticed this too. It's even been mentioned on some website articles.

Funny thing is, I can drive through the countryside and every white person in a pickup waves at me. Well, all I know is that it sure looks like a wave.

But it seems there's more whites than blacks who speak and wave at other people.

I used to get upset at the blacks who didn't speak or wave back at me. I don't anymore. I just say to myself, "Hey, that's cool," and move on.

That's because I thought about how I don't expect a white person or anyone else of another race who doesn't know me to speak. Why should I demand it from another black person? Saying hello is a courtesy, not an obligation. And quite honestly, there are some folks, black and white, I'm glad when they don't speak.

About the Author

Alonzo Weston joined the News-Press in 1989 as an intern. He currently covers social services and mental health and is also an award-winning columnist.

The St. Joseph native is a 2002 graduate of the inaugural class of the Diversity Institute at Vanderbilt University in Nashville, Tenn. He has been voted the city's favorite newspaper columnist for the past 20 years. He also has won numerous Missouri Press Association awards for his columns, features and investigative reporting.

He's been published in magazines and has had byline stories in the Nashville Tennessean and the New York Daily News.

Alonzo has served on the St. Joseph library board and is the chairman for the Knea-Von Black Archives and a research associate for the St. Joseph Museums Inc. He received the YWCA/NAACP Kelsy Beshears Racial Justice Award in 2005. The East Side Rotary Club also presented Alonzo with its Community Service Award in 2004. He received a Department of Mental Health Media Award in 2002 for a series of stories on local mental health issues.

Alonzo is active in the community in a number of ways. He and former News-Press opinion editor Mark Sheehan started the Coleman Hawkins Jazz Festival 12 years ago to honor the jazz legend and St. Joseph native.

The duo also created the Coleman Hawkins Mardi Gras Parade and blues festival and hosted an all-night youth basketball tournament to help raise funds for local community agencies.

Alonzo also created a journalism workshop for minority youth called Reporting L.I.V.E.

He and his wife, Deanna have two children, Alonzo Jr. and Nicole Hughes, a granddaughter, Asia Ann Weston, a grandson Jace Michael Deaver and a dog named Eubie.

Check out these books from
Amazing Things Press

Keeper of the Mountain by Nshan Erganian

Rare Blood Sect by Robert L. Justus

Survival In the Kitchen by Sharon Boyle

Stop Beating the Dead Horse by Julie L. Casey

In Daddy's Hands by Julie L. Casey

MariKay's Rainbow by Marilyn Weimer

Seeking the Green Flash by Lanny Daise

Thought Control by Robert L. Justus

Tales From Beneath the Crypt by Megan Marie

Fun Activities to Help Little Ones Talk by Kathy Blair

Bighorn by James Ozenberger

Post Exodus by Robert Christiansen

Rawnie's Mirage by Marilyn Weimer

All American Prizefighter by Rob Calloway

Fall of Grace by Rachel Riley and Sharon Spiegel

Taming the Whirlwind by Lindsey Heidle

Amazing Things Press

www.amazingthingspress.com

48882012R00133

Made in the USA
Lexington, KY
15 January 2016